A Promise Fulfilled

A Promise

FULFILLED

Theodor Herzl, Chaim Weizmann, David Ben-Gurion,
and the Creation of the State of Israel

Howard Greenfeld

Greenwillow Books
An Imprint of HarperCollins Publishers

A Promise Fulfilled: Theodor Herzl, Chaim Weizmann, and David Ben-Gurion, and the Creation of the State of Israel

Copyright © 2005 by Howard Greenfeld

All rights reserved. No part of this book may be used or reproduced in any manner whatsoever without written permission except in the case of brief quotations embodied in critical articles and reviews. Printed in the United States of America. For information address HarperCollins Children's Books, a division of HarperCollins Publishers, 1350 Avenue of the Americas, New York, NY 10019.

www.harperchildrens.com

Page 138 constitutes an extension of the copyright page.

The text of this book is set in Centaur.

Book design by Edward Miller

Library of Congress Cataloging-in-Publication Data

  Greenfeld, Howard.

A promise fulfilled : Theodor Herzl, Chaim Weizmann, and David Ben-Gurion, and the Creation of the State of Israel / by Howard Greenfeld.

    p. cm.

"Greenwillow Books."

ISBN 0-06-051504-X (trade). ISBN 0-06-051505-8 (lib. bdg.)

1. Zionists—Biography—Juvenile literature. 2. Zionism—History—Juvenile literature. 3. Herzl, Theodor, 1860–1904—Juvenile literature. 4. Weizmann, Chaim, 1874–1952—Juvenile literature. 5. Ben-Gurion, David, 1886–1973—Juvenile literature. I. Title.

DS151.A2G74 2005   320.54'095694'0922—dc22   2004054029

First Edition 10 9 8 7 6 5 4 3 2 1

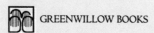 GREENWILLOW BOOKS

For Miriam and Jacob Shankman, with love

CONTENTS

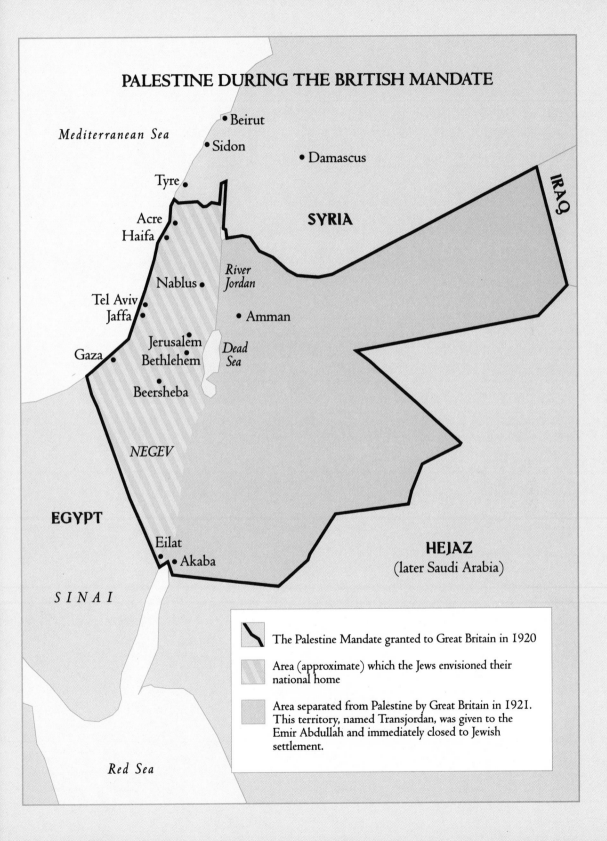

PALESTINE DURING THE BRITISH MANDATE

Mediterranean Sea

• Beirut

• Sidon

• Damascus

Tyre •

SYRIA

IRAQ

Acre •
Haifa •

Nablus •

River Jordan

Tel Aviv •
Jaffa •

• Amman

Jerusalem •
Bethlehem •

Dead Sea

Gaza •

Beersheba •

NEGEV

EGYPT

Eilat •
• Akaba

HEJAZ
(later Saudi Arabia)

SINAI

Red Sea

The Palestine Mandate granted to Great Britain in 1920

Area (approximate) which the Jews envisioned their national home

Area separated from Palestine by Great Britain in 1921. This territory, named Transjordan, was given to the Emir Abdullah and immediately closed to Jewish settlement.

INTRODUCTION

The promise referred to in the title of this book is the one God made to Abraham in the Book of Genesis to give him and his descendants "a great nation and a source of blessing to all." This history of the creation of the state of Israel tells the story of the fulfillment of that promise: the return of the Jews to the land of Israel, and the establishment of a state there.

Israel's conception at the First Zionist Congress in 1897 was remembered many years later by the distinguished Israeli statesman Abba Eban as an act of daring. "The effrontery of this intention is breathtaking: 197 delegates, purporting to represent millions of Jews, proposed, without the backing of any Jewish religious leaders or communal authorities and without the support of any of Western Europe's wealthiest and most influential leaders, to carve out of territories controlled by a hostile empire, a home in a land to which the Jews had not held title for some two thousand years," he wrote. And the five decades leading to the establishment of the state itself were filled with equally daring acts of courage, intelligence, and unflagging determination.

Ever since its birth in May 1948 the state of Israel has been at the center of the world's attention, inspiring both intense admiration and virulent anger. Some have even questioned the state's very right to exist.

I have written this short history because of the interest and frequently bitter controversy that this subject continues to generate and because of the surprising amount of ignorance displayed by many of those willing—and often eager—to discuss it. Anger or adoration too frequently replaces reason in these discussions.

In these pages I have tried to answer three basic questions: Why should the Jewish people have a state? Why did this state need to be located where it is? And why—and how—were they able to create this state? I believe that the answers to these questions can be found in the lives of three extraordinary men, as they lived them in relation to the creation of the state of Israel: Theodor Herzl, founder and first president of the World Zionist Organization; Chaim Weizmann, the first president of Israel; and David Ben-Gurion, Israel's first prime minister. All three were prominent among the many—far too many to mention in this introductory volume—who gave themselves to the struggle to fulfill a promise made thousands of years ago.

A Promise Fulfilled

CHAPTER 1

THEODOR HERZL

Born in Budapest, Hungary, on May 2, 1860
Died in Edlach, Austria, on July 3, 1904
Married Julie Naschauer in 1889
Daughter Pauline born in 1890
Son, Hans, born in 1891
Daughter Margarethe (Trude) born in 1893

THEODOR HERZL

"Diplomacy is the art of dealing with robbers."

No one person is more closely associated with the history of the state of Israel than Theodor Herzl. As founder and driving force of modern Zionism—the organized movement for the return of the Jews to their historic homeland of Palestine—Herzl laid the groundwork for the emergence, years after his death, of the modern Jewish state. This extraordinary man— brilliant, charismatic, a true visionary—has become a legendary figure, arguably the most important Jewish personality of the nineteenth century.

Nothing in his background would seem to indicate the direction Herzl's life would take or the distinction he would achieve. Born in Budapest on May 2, 1860, he spent the first eighteen years of his life in the Hungarian capital. His parents were well-to-do. His father, Jakob, though not born into wealth and with little formal education, became an affluent merchant and banker; his mother, Jeanette, came from an upper-class sophisticated world of wealth and culture. Both adored their children, Theodor and his older sister, Pauline.

Theodor was a precocious and unusually appealing child who was pampered by his parents. His upbringing may account for the self-confidence and arrogance that frequently characterized his behavior during his childhood and adolescence.

18

Drawing of Tabak Street, Budapest, Hungary, where Theodor Herzl was born in 1860

Although he was bright and intellectually curious, neither Judaism nor Jewish studies were among his interests in his early years. He was always aware that he was Jewish—he attended synagogue with his father (but not his mother, who showed no interest in religion), observed important Jewish holidays and customs, and celebrated his bar mitzvah—but the Herzls' life was not profoundly influenced or dominated by their Jewishness. They were assimilationists; they were among the many Jewish families who had adopted the customs as well as the language of the country in which they lived. In spite of this, Theodor soon learned that no matter how little he knew of his religious heritage, as a Jew he would inevitably be considered "different," an outsider in a non-Jewish world.

Believing that their son was advanced in every way, Theodor's doting parents hired a law student to tutor him and his sister, a year before he was required to attend grade school. Theodor was only five years old, and Pauline six. Many years later their tutor reminisced: "Within a short time both children made great strides in their studies. In less than two weeks they learned to read and write.... Theodor, especially, absorbed things very easily and excelled with his quick power of perception. Only a few weeks after he started to study he composed a little speech in which he expressed happy new year wishes to his parents in German as well as in French...." The boy's charm also attracted public attention. During the walks he took with his sister and their tutor, strangers—especially young women—were drawn to him and tried to engage him in conversation.

Theodor's formal schooling began in the fall of 1866, when he entered grade school. It was a Jewish school; the large majority of the students were Jewish, and among the subjects were "Biblical Hebrew" and "Religious Studies." Theodor did well in both subjects, for which he had had no preparation, and also received outstanding grades in Hungarian, German, science, and mathematics. After four years there (Jewish schools did not go beyond the fourth grade), his parents sent him to *Realschule*, a six-year technical school that put great emphasis on science and mathematics. This decision to send him to a technical school rather than to a traditional eight-year *Gymnasium* (high school), which emphasized the humanities and prepared its students for continuing studies at a university, is difficult to explain, except perhaps by his parents' mistaken belief that Theodor's great interest in technical subjects in elementary school was more serious—and permanent—than it actually was.

Whatever the reason, the decision to send the ten-year-old to *Realschule* was not wise; he didn't like the school or his classes. Nonetheless, the time he spent there proved to be most significant for two reasons, both of value in determining his future: the realization that he had lost interest in science led to his real interest, a career as a writer, and his awareness of anti-Semitism at school—anti-Jewish humor, the exclusion of Jews from certain activities, etcetera—brought home the evil he would have to confront for the rest of his life. In an article written many years later, he linked the two. "I soon lost my former love for logarithms and trigonometry, because a distinctly anti-Semitic trend prevailed at the technical high school. One of our teachers explained the meaning of the word 'heathen' as referring to idolators, Mohammedans, and Jews. After that peculiar definition I was fed up with this school and wanted to transfer to a classical *Gymnasium*."

In spite of his determination to leave the *Realschule*, Theodor did not officially enter a *Gymnasium* until the fall of 1875. Before then he attended the technical school only sporadically, taking months off to study at home, most often with a tutor, so that he would be prepared for his classes at his new school. It was not a happy time. He was restless and lonely; he had no close friends. His grades, a reflection of his discontent, were poor—somewhat startling for a teenager (he had turned thirteen in 1873) who had earlier shown such great promise.

His last years at the *Realschule* were not entirely wasted, however, for it was then that young Herzl decided to become a writer. He was so devoted to this goal that he spent many of his hours—at the science-oriented school and away from it—writing. He had from early childhood been a voracious reader and demonstrated a precocious gift for languages, so it was not surprising that his enthusiasm for reading should, as he entered adolescence, be transformed into a passion for writing.

Herzl not only liked to write but also enjoyed having his work read and admired. He was so sure of his talent that in February 1874, in order to reach as many interested readers as possible, he and four or five other boys his age founded a literary society named WIR ("we"), which would publicly criticize the writings of its own members. It was rigidly organized, and its purpose precisely defined: The statutes called for the "founding of an association dedicated to enriching our knowledge by writing short stories or fairy tales which would enhance our mastery of the language."

Herzl, who was officially elected president of the small group (he firmly believed in formal organization), dominated all its meetings. Basking in the praise of his fellow members, he led the discussions—largely of his own short stories, essays, and poetry, which dealt with such weighty themes as heroism (two of his special heroes were Napoleon and Martin Luther), mythology, and obedience.

The literary society lasted for only two months. It was rumored that members disapproved of their president's dictatorial leadership. Whether or not that was the case, the principal reason the group disbanded was that the work done for WIR interfered with the members' academic studies. Herzl himself never considered the demise of WIR a failure. On the contrary, his literary output during its short existence merely confirmed what he already believed: that his future success as a writer was assured.

Herzl's move to *Gymnasium* a short time before his fifteenth birthday was a success. His academic work improved. He was not an ideal student—his grades were inconsistent, and he was frequently unprepared for class—but he managed to maintain a decent grade average throughout his years at the school.

Not surprisingly, he was increasingly immersed in his writing, which took up far too much of his time and most probably accounted for his undistinguished academic performance.

The amount of time he put into his literary work, however, was justified by the results of his efforts. His style and fluency improved steadily, and he was soon submitting mature essays and short sketches to magazines and newspapers. To his delight, some of these were accepted for publication—not only because of the young author's skill but also because of his persistence. He knew he was a talented writer, and he was determined that others recognize his talent.

Though his social life improved at the *Gymnasium*—emboldened by his taste of success as a writer, he was no longer isolated from the other students—the young man was not liked by all his classmates. He could be arrogant, overbearing, and sarcastic. But he could also be good company, and his wit and mischievous pranks and jokes managed to endear him to a number of his fellow students, none of whom could doubt his keen intelligence and astounding memory.

22

In February 1878, Herzl's childhood and adolescence ended abruptly. After an illness of only three days his beloved nineteen-year-old sister died of typhus. Almost the same age, he and Pauline had been more than just siblings; they had been the closest of friends. Herzl was heartbroken, as were his parents. In an unpublished sketch, the young man described the "horrible night" of his sister's death: "I sat talking with my mother and a few aunts, while my father sat at the deathbed of my sister, my beloved Pauline. Suddenly we heard loud sobbing in the sickroom, an unforgettable sound such as only the cruel blow of fate's hammer on a father's twitching heart can evoke. We knew she was dead. . . . My mother did not cry. Later on she cried for several years, incessantly. The capacity of a mother's tear glands is beyond belief, enough to fill an ocean. I shed a lot of tears, and then I fell asleep. I was now my parents' only child."

In that same unpublished memoir, Herzl described the funeral: "My

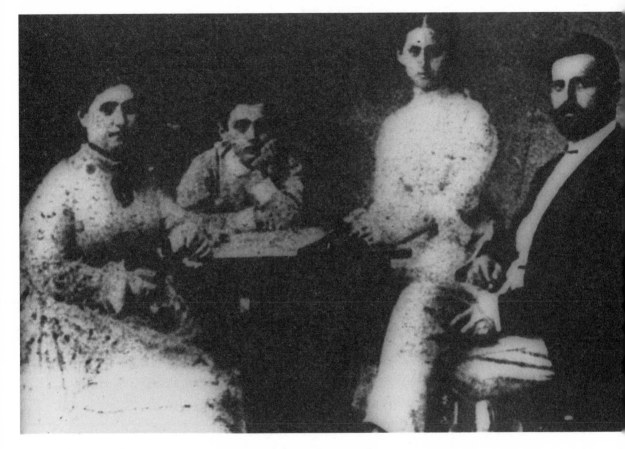

Theodor Herzl with his parents and sister, Pauline, Budapest, Hungary, 1873

father, mother, and I slowly walked behind the slow-moving hearse. In it lay my dead sister, whose mouth I would never again seal with a brotherly kiss to make up after a mock quarrel. I vaguely felt how hard that was going to be, but the people by the wayside stopped to watch us, and somehow that seemed to comfort me a little as I led my father by the arm. He stumbled along, all but doubled over, and he has remained so ever since. And then we stood at the edge of the square hole, and with uncanny speed the gravediggers did their job. . . . They put my beloved only sister into the cold earth, one who had been so used to drift in comfort through a well-heated life, that sweet, young blood. Now she was to lie all alone, outside the city, in wind and storm and rain, she who never even crossed the street by herself. That was hard. Even for me. I dimly began to feel it. Why did you do that? Why did you die?"

Unable to live among the memories that Budapest now held for them, the Herzls moved to Vienna, less than one week after Pauline's death. Jakob had considered making such a move even before the family's tragic loss. He believed both his beloved children, approaching maturity, would have more professional opportunities in the Austrian capital than in Budapest. Moreover, having suffered serious financial setbacks in Budapest, he thought he could just as easily make a living away from the Hungarian capital as in it.

Surprisingly, given the pain he continued to suffer following Pauline's death, Theodor adapted to life in the Austrian capital with enthusiasm. Vienna's charm was apparently irresistible. Compared with Budapest, it was enormously vital, a bustling city of music and art and splendid, elegant baroque architecture. It also offered a warm welcome to its Jewish population, which had grown steadily from six thousand in 1859 to seventy-three thousand in 1880.

In the spring of 1878, soon after settling in Vienna, Herzl enrolled in the law school of the University of Vienna. He had never shown any interest in becoming a lawyer—he remained determined to become a writer—but his parents believed that it would be wise for their son to have a law degree in case he failed to succeed in his chosen field.

Though in the beginning Herzl showed little distinction as a writer—and even less as a law student—he made his presence known in Vienna's social circles. Self-assured and striking in appearance, he cut an aristocratic figure and was accepted wherever he went. Although he could seem cool and distant,

Opposite page: Theodor Herzl *(far right)* in 1882 as a member of the student union at the University of Vienna

he was a young man of considerable charm and earned a reputation for his sharp wit, refined manners, and impeccable taste. He also knew how to have a good time and became known for his taste for beer and gambling.

His carefree life in Vienna soon changed, however. Anti-Semitism, in the form of books, newspaper articles, and political pronouncements, was rising to the surface once again. The "Jewish problem" was being blamed for a severe economic crisis, which was spreading throughout much of Europe.

At first, Herzl was able to minimize the seriousness of this "problem." He believed there was no "Jewish problem" that could not be solved by assimilating the Jews into the Christian community. Gradually, however, this pervasive anti-Semitism began to affect him personally. By 1883 it had started to sweep over the entire university and reached the leaders of his college fraternity. They publicly sided against the Jews in a dispute between different factions in the fraternity. Herzl issued an angry protest that, when rejected, was followed by his resignation from the organization. This was a significant move—his first public stand against the injustices that faced all Jews—not only in Vienna but throughout Europe.

Herzl completed his studies with little enthusiasm and became a Doctor of Law in 1884. He worked for a short time as a civil servant in Vienna and Salzburg, but he soon realized that he could never pursue a career in the law. By August 1885 he had made up his mind to devote his life to the written word: to literature, to ideas, and to his special passion, the theater.

With enormous energy and flair, he made it clear that what he sought above all was widespread recognition and popular approval, commercial rather than literary success. With the financial and emotional support of his parents, he was able to devote all his time to achieving his goal. He wrote essays and stories and criticism and travel sketches, for the most part clever and light

and whimsical pieces that before long were professional enough to be published in newspapers and magazines in Vienna and Berlin, two of Europe's
most sophisticated cities. Many of these articles and stories were known as
feuilletons, brief commentaries on the social and cultural events of the period.
They earned him the public he wanted and, in time, the reputation he eagerly
sought. He also wrote plays that were produced with varying degrees of success throughout Europe and even in America. His plays, together with the
published collections of his stories and articles, made his name familiar and
respected throughout the Continent.

He was best known, however, for his journalism, and in 1891, after having
held editorial posts on a number of prominent publications, he was appointed
Paris correspondent for Vienna's finest and most powerful liberal newspaper,
Neue Freie Presse. By accepting this important position, the thirty-one-year-old
journalist was realizing two of his goals: His words and ideas would be read
and listened to by Vienna's—and perhaps Europe's—most influential public,
and he was being given the opportunity to live in Paris, a city he had learned to
love in the course of several visits.

The French capital was then the lively cultural and political center of
Europe, and the ambitious young journalist took advantage of all the wonders
it had to offer. A successful writer, charming, elegant, urbane, and unusually
attractive, he easily fitted in with the artists, writers, and intellectuals who
brought the city to life. His perspective was enriched and broadened while
there. He studied French and European history, and he became expert in
contemporary French affairs. There was only one negative aspect to his assignment there, but it was serious. He was forced to recognize, far more than ever
before, the growing threat that anti-Semitism posed to the Jews of France as
well as to those living elsewhere.

While in Vienna, Herzl had underestimated the significance of this anti-Semitism, believing that it was a temporary blight that would somehow go away. In Paris he learned that this had been a serious miscalculation.

His first article on a Jewish matter—specifically about French anti-Semitism—was published in *Neue Freie Presse.* It was little more than a rather mild, occasionally sarcastic social commentary, but it was an important turning point in Herzl's life. It signaled the beginning of what became his persistent quest for a solution to the complex question—the fate of the Jews—that soon, he wrote, "gnawed and tugged at me, it tormented me and rendered me profoundly unhappy."

Herzl's previously held belief that the answer to the Jewish question was the complete assimilation—really, the disappearance—of Jews within the non-Jewish majority now seemed unworkable and unsatisfactory. The idea had led him in many directions, even, in 1895, to ponder an extraordinary scheme that called for the mass baptism in Vienna of the Jewish population of Austria. He noted the details in his diary:

> The conversion was to take place in broad daylight, Sundays at noon in St. Stephen's Cathedral, with a solemn procession and the ringing of bells. Not furtively, the way individual Jews had gone about it until then, but in dignified pride. And because the leaders would take their people only up to the gates of the church while themselves remaining Jews, the whole enterprise would attain a level of great sincerity. We who stood firm would have marked the last generation, still clinging to [the] faith of our forefathers. But we wanted to make Christians of our young sons before they reached the age of reason, at which point conversion smacks of

cowardice. As usual I had worked out the entire plan to the most minute detail. In my mind's eye I already saw myself dealing with the Archbishop of Vienna, facing the Pope—both of whom regretted my decision to remain with the Jews—and bringing to the world this message of racial fusion.

He soon realized the absurdity of this bizarre plan. Though reared as an assimilated Jew himself, he also soon came to understand that no form of assimilation or conversion would serve as a satisfactory solution to the Jewish question. In the eyes of the anti-Semites, a blood Jew, inherently evil, remained a Jew, even after conversion.

The situation was far more complex than he had realized, and it called for a more effective and feasible—as well as far more daring—solution. To reach it, he set about studying the condition of the Jews throughout the world. He did so thoroughly and meticulously, and his findings confirmed his fears that the need for an answer was urgent and dramatic.

Herzl found problems for the Jewish population in every part of Europe. The most disturbing were those faced by the Jews of Russia, who for many years had been, with the consent and encouragement of the Russian government, victims of pogroms (organized persecutions or massacres). Most Russian Jews were forced to live in abject poverty under the fear of rape, murder, and expulsion. Those who had survived had been deprived of their fundamental rights—the right to the employment of their choice, to the residence of their choice, to the education of their choice—by a series of anti-Semitic laws. These cruel laws forced thousands to flee their homes in search of freedom and refuge outside Russia. A mass exodus began in 1881 and 1882, after which an average of fifty to sixty thousand Jews left each year. Some one hundred thousand Jews left Russia in 1891, and more than one hundred and thirty-seven thousand the following year.

Closer to home, in France, Herzl was personally aware of widespread and all-too-frequent harassment of Jews. He was also profoundly disturbed by the French government's behavior abroad, especially by its growing support for the viciously anti-Semitic Russian government. At the same time, anti-Semitism was increasing even in Austria, where a government openly hostile to the Jews was coming to power.

No single event can account for what has been called Herzl's emotional explosion—his determination to improve the plight of the beleaguered Jewish people—yet the widely reported case of Captain Alfred Dreyfus, an unjustly accused Jewish officer in the French Army, certainly intensified his awareness of the need for action.

This infamous case, which shook France and the rest of the Western world, began in 1894, when a French spy at the German embassy in Paris came across an unsigned letter, with an appended memorandum, listing documents that revealed French military secrets. The memorandum was obviously meant for the German military attaché. An intense search for the traitor who had prepared it followed, and the army finally accused Captain Dreyfus, a wealthy Jewish officer with a spotless record, who worked at the War Office. Though he vigorously protested his innocence, Dreyfus, apparently a victim of anti-Semitism, was court-martialed in December 1894 and condemned to life in solitary confinement on Devil's Island, a penal colony in French Guiana. Herzl covered the trial as a reporter. Two weeks later, in January 1895, he stood in a freezing Parisian courtyard and watched, in horror, a ceremony in which the framed Jewish officer (who was later fully exonerated) was publicly degraded. Stripped of his rank and drummed out of the army, Dreyfus was led away in disgrace, as an angry mob shouted, "Death to the Jews!" Few doubted that his religion accounted for the verdict.

Only six months later, in the first entry of a political diary he kept for the rest of his life, Herzl dramatically announced the cause that obsessed him until his death:

> I have become occupied for some time past with a work which is of immeasurable greatness. I cannot tell today whether I shall bring it to a close. It has the appearance of a gigantic dream. But for days and weeks it has filled me, saturated even my subconsciousness; it accompanies me wherever I go, broods above my ordinary daily converse, looks over my shoulder and at my petty, comical journalistic work. It disturbs me, and intoxicates me.
>
> What it will lead to is impossible to surmise as yet. But my experience tells me that it is something marvelous, even as a dream, and that I should write it down—if not as a memorial for mankind, then for my own delight or meditation in later years. And perhaps for something between both these possibilities: for the enrichment of literature. If the romance does not become a fact, at least the fact can become a romance. Title: The Promised Land!

With these words, the handsome, elegant journalist and man-about-town—heretofore known for his witty and entertaining articles—began his transformation into a brilliant, tireless, and dynamic leader, consumed by a single cause: the search for a solution to the Jewish question.

Having absorbed what he had learned from his travels and subsequent

The Jews' claim to the land called Israel has its roots in the biblical story of God's promise to Abraham to make him and his descendants "a great nation and a source of blessing to all nations" (Genesis 12:2–3) in a territory called Canaan. Years later, in order to escape a drought that was ravaging Canaan, the people of Israel (the name God had chosen for Abraham's grandson Jacob when he renewed his promise of the land to him, Genesis 35:11–12) found refuge in Egypt. At first they prospered, but when their population grew, they were enslaved by the Egyptians, who feared they would ally themselves with Egypt's enemies. Generations later, under Moses' command, the Israelites revolted, and with God's help they fled Egypt. It took the twelve tribes constituting the Israelites forty years to reach the promised land, "a land flowing with milk and honey" (Genesis 33:1–3).

The Israelites thrived. They conquered Canaan and established a kingdom. King David founded its capital, Jerusalem, on Mount Zion, and his successor, Solomon, built the first temple. The Jews (named after David's tribe, Judah) faced many enemies over the centuries and in 586 BCE

were defeated by the Babylonians, who conquered Jerusalem, burned the temple, and exiled the Jews to Babylon. The Jews, however, never severed their ties to their land: "by the rivers of Babylon, there we sat down; yea we wept when we remembered Zion" (Psalm 137).

In 538 BCE the Persians defeated the Babylonians and allowed the Jews to return to Zion, thus ending the first exile. The Jews rebuilt the temple and resumed their lives in Israel. Centuries later, in 70 CE, the Romans vanquished the Jews and destroyed the second temple. The Jews were enslaved and exiled again. The Romans changed the name of Israel to Palestine, after the Philistines, the enemy who King David had defeated a thousand years earlier. Remnants of Jewish communities lived on in the holy cities of Hebron, Safed, Tiberius, and, of course, Jerusalem. But most were scattered around the known world. This time the exile lasted 1,878 years (70 CE to 1948 CE), but all that time the Jews remained emotionally tied to Jerusalem. Jews faced toward Jerusalem during prayers, and at the end of the Passover celebration the phrase "Next year in Jerusalem" sustained that hope for almost two thousand years.

studies, Herzl had already reached the conclusion that there was only one feasible solution: The Jews, having for centuries been scorned, discriminated against, and eventually forced to leave the lands in which they lived as second-class citizens, could, he believed, be assured of their well-being only through the establishment of a separate country of their own. They needed a Jewish territory with an independent Jewish government. Herzl himself was prepared to play the leading role in the practical realization of this bold dream. He was also more than eager—he felt he was destined—to become the leader of a modern Zionist movement whose goal would be the return of the Jewish people to their historic birthplace, then known as Palestine.

It was a daunting mission that would call for an enormous amount of courage and money. Land suitable for habitation and cultivation by many thousands of Jews would have to be found and purchased. Once the land had been acquired, the exodus of Jews from many parts of the world would have to be carefully planned, along with their settlement in their new territory. In spite of the difficulties Herzl knew he would face, he was confident that he could achieve his goal. Driven by a cause in which he believed profoundly, he would need all his intelligence and ingenuity—as a skilled politician, as a charismatic personality with a flair for the theatrical, and as a gifted man of letters—in order to lead his people to their salvation.

At the first step, Herzl spent the second half of 1895 traveling—to Vienna, Berlin, Paris, and London—in an effort to gain financial support for his plan from Europe's wealthiest Jews. It was a difficult trip, and despite his great powers of persuasion, his efforts to raise the sums of money needed were in most cases disappointing. He met setbacks everywhere. Members of the immensely affluent Rothschild family, who could have easily financed his work, turned him down; they had already established colonies of their own and planned to continue establishing them in Palestine. Another potential donor,

33

Baron Maurice de Hirsch, who had amassed a fortune in railroads and whose ostentatious home intimidated Herzl, had already donated a huge amount of money toward the settlement of Russian Jews in the spacious farmlands of Argentina, and furthermore, had nothing but contempt for Herzl's methods and ideas. Their conversation was uncomfortable and unfriendly. Other meetings were equally unsuccessful. To Herzl's dismay, most of those to whom he enthusiastically outlined his ideas were, he wrote, "utterly oblivious of the danger I then foresaw."

HERZL'S PREDECESSORS

Theodor Herzl was not the first proponent of a Jewish homeland. The longing for a return to their land sustained the Jews in the Diaspora (the dispersion of Jews outside Israel) for two thousand years.

At the end of the eighteenth century, as the result of the French Revolution, Jews throughout Europe started to gain civil rights, and these changes engendered a new sense of national ambition. Enlightened Jews started to express their opinions on their need for a homeland where Jews would be safe and where their religion, culture, and customs could be openly practiced.

Among them was Moses Hess, a former collaborator of Marx and Engels's who expressed these beliefs in a book, *Rome and Jerusalem*, published in 1862. Similarly, and independently, Leo Pinsker in 1882 published a pamphlet, *Autoemancipation*, advocating the foundation of a national Jewish homeland. Starting in 1868, Perez Smolenskin combated both orthodoxy and assimilation, extolling the Hebrew language and espousing the return to the homeland, in his monthly publication *HaShachar* ("The Dawn").

And following the pogroms in Russia in 1881, a group of Russian Jews started the Hovevei Zion movement to pursue the goal of a Jewish homeland in Palestine.

In the face of his failure to arouse interest in his plan among the wealthy and powerful Jewish leaders of Europe, Herzl chose another tactic. He wrote down his ideas in a statement that might eventually reach people—not only the rich but also the poor, Jewish and non-Jewish, all over the world. He first put these ideas into a long letter to Baron de Hirsch, who was no more receptive to them in writing than he had been during their face-to-face meeting. Unwilling to accept failure, Herzl then prepared an expanded version of his ideas for the Rothschild family. Finally he decided to write an even longer version, a definitive one, this time for publication. Working feverishly, he completed it during the winter of 1895–1896. The result was a pamphlet of some twenty-three thousand words that he titled *Der Judenstaat (The Jewish State: An Attempt at a Modern Solution of the Jewish Question)*. It is one of the basic documents of Zionist literature and answers the question of why there is a need for a Jewish state.

The author's purpose is stated clearly in the preface: "The idea which I have developed in this pamphlet is an ancient one: It is the restoration of the Jewish State. . . . The decisive factor is our propelling force. And what is that force? The plight of the Jews. . . . I am profoundly convinced that I am right, though I doubt whether I shall live to see myself proved so. Those today who inaugurate this movement are unlikely to live to see its glorious culmination. But the very inauguration is enough to inspire in them a high pride and the joy of an inner liberation of their existence."

Herzl continues with a well-considered analysis of the Jewish question—not (as was usually the case) as a religious or a social but as a national question, with a national solution.

We are a people—one people. We have sincerely tried everywhere to merge with the national communities in which we live, seeking only to preserve the faith of our fathers. It is not permitted us.

In vain are we loyal patriots, sometimes superloyal; in vain do we make the same sacrifices of life and property as our fellow citizens; in vain do we strive to advance the fame of our native lands in the arts and sciences, or her wealth by trade and commerce. In our native lands where we have lived for centuries we are still decried as aliens, often by men whose ancestors had not yet come at a time when Jewish sighs had long been heard in the country. The majority decide who the "alien" is. . . .

Oppression and persecution cannot exterminate us. No nation on earth has endured such struggles and sufferings as we have. Jew-baiting has merely winnowed out our weaklings; the strong among us defiantly return to our own whenever persecution breaks out. . . .

No human being is wealthy or powerful enough to transplant a people from one place of residence to another. Only an idea can achieve that. The State surely has that power. The Jews have dreamed this princely dream throughout the long night of their history. "Next year in Jerusalem" is our age-old motto. It is now a matter of showing that the vague dream can be transformed into a clear and glowing idea.

Herzl concludes on an optimistic note: "Let me repeat once more my opening words. The Jews who will it shall achieve their State. We shall live at last as free men on our own soil, and in our own homes peacefully die. The world will be liberated by our freedom, enriched by our wealth, magnified by our greatness. And whatever we shall attempt there for our own benefit will redound mightily and beneficially to the good of all mankind."

Herzl's sixty-four-page pamphlet aroused controversy, among both Jews and non-Jews. Many Jews were indignant; they had for many years worked hard to become recognized as full citizens of the European countries in which they lived, and they believed that by establishing a new Jewish state, thereby recognizing their separateness, they would be endangering the rights they had fought for and finally achieved at home. Others thought that Herzl was attempting to usurp God's role in bringing about the coming of the Messiah and the return of the Jews to their land. Still others believed that Herzl was simply a madman whose ideas were wild, impractical ravings. A number of readers, however, whether or not they agreed with all of the author's ideas, recognized that *The Jewish State* was an honest, forthright argument for Zionism by a distinguished journalist and an astute political observer.

Many of those who saw the merits of Herzl's ideas helped him arrange meetings with a number of prominent figures—members of the non-Jewish nobility, political leaders, and wealthy Jews, especially in France and England—who could help him raise money to implement his ambitious plans. But as had happened before the publication of his pamphlet, he was, for the most part, rebuffed in his efforts to gain followers.

Still, Herzl did not give up. Instead he again changed his strategy. He took his message to the working people whose political meetings he addressed at every opportunity and who responded with increasing enthusiasm.

His unexpected success was astounding. His ideas and his fame spread rapidly. Responses—telegrams and letters—arrived from all over the world: Bulgaria, Galicia, Palestine, even Russia, where *The Jewish State* had been banned but had been smuggled in. Many of his new supporters urged him to lead them. Some had come to consider him the new Moses. On the way to Vienna from Constantinople (now Istanbul), he was greeted at the train station in Sofia, Bulgaria, by a mob and carried triumphantly to a synagogue, where he was hailed as the Messiah.

By the time this trip came to an end, Herzl had spent a huge amount of his own money. But he stubbornly believed that he was on his way to a victory, that his goal would soon be reached.

Of all the gatherings he attended, none was as moving as that held on July 13, 1896, at the Jewish Workingmen's Club in London's East End. The audience who filled the hall on a hot Sunday afternoon consisted largely of workers—poor Eastern European refugees, most of them from Russia and Romania—and Herzl's reception was vividly described by one of his followers, a twenty-five-year-old journalist, Jakob de Haas: "Herzl, who less than a year before sought only the good will and support of millionaires, was suddenly changed into the spearhead of a phalanx rebelling against the existing Jewish communal organization. . . . The masses surged into the meeting hall, into which only a tithe of the sweltering crowd could gain admission. Herzl was no orator of the masses and amid all that jubilation he permitted himself only one sentence that had the savour of triumph. He said, 'The East is ours,' meaning the East End of London. But his personality, his glowing eyes, his fine simple gestures, his deprecating of himself and the natural touch of mystery with which he spoke of diplomatic affairs, won an audience. . . ."

Herzl was overwhelmed by the reception to his extemporaneous one-hour speech and by the wild cheering that followed him out of the auditorium. It was a turning point and a new direction in his struggle for Zionism, and he wrote in his diary a few days later:

> As I sat on the platform of the Workingmen's stage I underwent a curious experience. I saw and heard my legend being made. The people are sentimental; the masses do not see clearly. I believe that by now they no longer have a clear image of me. A faint mist is

beginning to rise and envelop me, and may perhaps become the cloud in which I shall walk.

But even if they no longer see my features distinctly, still they sense that I mean truly well by them and that I am the little people's man. . . .

Perhaps the most interesting thing I am recording in this book: how my own legend is being born.

And while I was listening, on that people's tribune, to the fulsome words and cheering of my adherents, I made a firm and silent resolve to become even worthier of their trust and love.

Though he was of course cheered and encouraged by his glowing reception as the "champion of the poor," Herzl was a realist. He believed he would have to continue his efforts to find support from the wealthy, and he turned, albeit reluctantly, to Edmond de Rothschild, another member of the Rothschild family, who agreed to meet with him in Paris. However, once again Herzl was rebuffed, rudely and at far greater length this time. Humiliated and enraged by his angry two-hour meeting with Rothschild, Herzl finally concluded that he could never rely upon help from the wealthy. He was now convinced that it was essential to expand his efforts and to mobilize with equal energy all those—the poor as well as the rich—who shared his ambitious goals.

He was prepared to begin at once. As a first step he saw the need to bring together a large number of men and women—dissimilar in many ways but with a common dream—into a single formal international organization. With characteristic dedication and energy, he set to work: he rented an office, hired a staff, prepared and published circulars and pamphlets, sought speaking engagements wherever possible, maintained a huge correspondence, and received visitors with whom to exchange ideas.

In a remarkably short time—January 1897, only six months after delivering his speech at the Workingmen's Club in London—he was ready to take a significant and bold step forward: to convene the first meeting of Zionists the following summer. To organize such an enormous undertaking, a demonstration of national solidarity that would stimulate the imagination of Jews everywhere and empower their political representatives, was a gigantic task, but Herzl achieved it, largely with his own labor as well as his own money.

Because of this one man's efforts, the First Zionist Congress, the first Jewish parliamentary body in modern history, convened on the morning of

Theodor Herzl *(center, at podium)* addresses the First Zionist Congress in Basel, Switzerland, in 1897; Herzl and the delegates wear formal attire

August 29, 1897, to discuss the future of the Jews. On that morning the great hall of the stately Municipal Casino in Basel, Switzerland, was crowded with some two hundred Zionist delegates from seventeen countries as well as members of the public and journalists from all over the world. To emphasize the unique significance and seriousness of the opening session, Herzl decreed that all delegates wear formal clothes: black frock coats and white ties. His experience as a dramatist had not been wasted.

Theodor Herzl gives a speech at the First Zionist Congress

The gathering was a tremendous personal triumph for Herzl. Remembering his own experience on that historic occasion, Dr. Mayer Ebner, at the time a young Zionist, wrote more than a half century later:

> Herzl's appearance at the solemn opening session of the First Congress has forever remained vivid in my memory. He was welcomed with an enthusiasm as I have never witnessed again in so many important national and international congresses in which I participated in later years. Theodor Herzl stood before us, pale and with lowered head, acclaimed by applause which hardly abated. He had not yet uttered a word, yet all of us were spellbound by the majesty of his personality and of his extraordinary mission. Not a few

41

of us—as they freely admitted later—believed in those moments of ecstasy to behold the bodily Messiah, the Saviour of Israel.

Many wept. My eyes too were filled with tears. One of the secrets of Herzl's influence was his unusual manly beauty which deeply impressed even the mighty of the earth. Even now, when fully awake, I sometimes still see Herzl in front of me and hear the ring of his voice. Never to be obliterated from my memory is the content of his addresses, which introduced a new epoch of Jewish history and which will always remain a masterpiece of his noble style.

In his opening address, Herzl declared, in a few words, that the purpose of the congress was "to lay the foundation stone of the house which is to shelter the Jewish nation." He noted that this was now possible because modern means of communication had for the first time enabled the dispersed elements of the Jewish people to come together, and he declared that it was a responsibility of Zionists to seek to awaken Jewish people in every part of the world.

The emotionally charged meeting lasted for only three days, but it accomplished an enormous amount: Zionism emerged as a unified movement with a leader, a program, and an organization. The leader was of course Herzl. The program (later known as the Basel Program) defined the goal of Zionism: "to create for the Jewish people a publicly and legally assured home in Palestine." And finally, the delegates established a permanent organization to cope with the complexities of the Jewish question. It was to include all Jews who accepted the Zionist program and to be known as the World Zionist Organization. Its first president was Herzl.

Opposite page: Theodor Herzl in Basel, during the First Zionist Congress, on the balcony of the Three Kings Hotel

The final session of the First Zionist Congress, on August 31, 1897, concluded on a note of optimism. There were cheers of satisfaction and pledges of loyalty as well as assurances of more such gatherings to come.

Herzl himself was well aware of the profound significance of those few days. On September 3 he wrote in his diary: "In Basel, I founded the Jewish state. If I were to say that aloud today, everyone would laugh at me. Maybe in five years, but certainly in fifty, everyone will agree."

The founder and moving spirit of modern Zionism remained president of the World Zionist Organization and presided over all Zionist congresses until his death. The meetings were held annually and each lasted three or four days. The number of delegates grew steadily (some 200 attended the first one while 592 attended the sixth, Herzl's last) and as it did, the congress attracted an increasing number of journalists, who publicized the work of the organization and helped establish Zionism as a social and political force not only in Europe but throughout the world. In a short time, Zionism became legitimate.

A number of challenges confronted the delegates to the congresses, and the issues they debated during the long, intense, and often heated discussions were many and complex. They were only at the very beginning of the long road that would lead, as Herzl predicted, to the creation of a new state. Although many of these discussions dealt with issues affecting the growing number of local Zionist organizations, most concerned the details involved in establishing a homeland for the Jewish people in Palestine.

First of all, it was necessary to locate, negotiate for, and then purchase the land to be used by the settlers. Most of this land was owned by wealthy Arabs, the majority of whom lived outside of Palestine—in Cairo, Damascus, and Beirut. Furthermore, banks and other financial institutions had to be established to accommodate the needs of the pioneers. In addition, there was the matter of moving the Jews from the lands in which they had been oppressed (the majority

THE OTTOMAN EMPIRE

Palestine had become part of the vast and powerful Ottoman (or Turkish) Empire in 1516–17. The empire, named after its Turkish founder, Osman, had grown steadily for several centuries. In the late thirteenth century the Ottomans ruled over a small state in Asia Minor; their rule extended rapidly into Europe and the Middle East. By the middle of the fifteenth century they had conquered large areas of Greece and the Balkans. In 1453 Constantinople, which was the capital of the Byzantine Empire, was captured and became the capital of the Ottoman Empire.

The power of the empire reached its peak in the sixteenth century, when its southern border extended from the Persian Gulf to Morocco and its northern borders from the Crimea to the eastern approaches to Vienna. In 1516–17 Palestine was seized from the Egyptian Mamelukes (originally slaves from Turkey, they had occupied Palestine for two hundred years), and it became a part of the empire until the end of World War I.

from Eastern Europe) into the land in which they had chosen to live. Organization of the new settlements too was of great concern—not only socially and economically but also culturally, artistically, and educationally.

Herzl was, as he demanded to be, at the center of all these activities. He worked tirelessly during the annual conventions and between them. In the autumn of 1898 he paid his first visit to Palestine, where he stayed for only a few weeks. At the end of the trip he wrote in his diary: "When I remember thee in days to come, O Jerusalem, it will not be with delight. The musty deposits of two thousand years of inhumanity, intolerance, and foulness lie in your reeking alleys. The one man who has been present here all this while, the lovable dreamer of Nazareth, has done nothing but help increase the hate."

Opposite page: Theodor Herzl en route to Israel, 1898. *Above:* Theodor Herzl and a Zionist delegation visit Jerusalem, 1898.

Convinced that personal diplomacy was essential to achieve the Zionists' goals, Herzl traveled from one country to another, seeking and usually gaining audiences with some of Europe's most powerful leaders. He sought political and economic support for his cause, but the results were almost always disappointing. His powers of persuasion fell short. Although he was received politely and with respect, he came away from these meetings with no offers of assistance.

Most disappointing of all was his experience with Sultan Abdul Hamid II, then the Turkish ruler of Palestine, from whom it would be most important to obtain a legal charter for the Jewish state. The sultan hosted Herzl at an elaborate banquet, and the two men held a friendly two-hour conversation. Once again, however, the Zionist leader failed; after complex negotiations no agreement was reached.

He was similarly rebuffed in his efforts to win support from Europe's wealthy Jewish communities. "I have run myself ragged, and I haven't obtained a hearing from the wretched crew which controls the money," he wrote bitterly in his diary in 1901. "It is something utterly unheard of and fifty years from now people will spit on the graves of these men." He was physically and emotionally tired, and he was discouraged. In another diary entry, he said: "I feel my autumn approaching and see before me the danger of leaving no achievements to the world."

Theodor Herzl rides in a horse-drawn carriage, Izmir, Turkey, 1898

It was in this condition of near despair that Herzl was forced to deal with the greatest crisis to date in the history of the organized Zionist movement. In May 1903 Joseph Chamberlain, colonial secretary of Great Britain, mentioned to Herzl that a large area of British-controlled land in East Africa (mistakenly identified as Uganda, it is now within the boundaries of Kenya) would make an ideal location for a Jewish settlement. Though Chamberlain assumed that the climate on the coast would be too hot for European settlers, he believed the interior would be ideal, suited as it was for the planting of sugar and cotton. Herzl initially rejected the offer, insisting that the Jews would accept nothing less than a settlement in Palestine. Then a vicious pogrom in the Russian city of Kishinev, in which forty-five Jews were killed, eighty-six wounded, and more than fifteen hundred Jewish houses and shops destroyed, made the Zionist leader change his mind. Realizing that the very future of Russian Jewry was endangered, Herzl decided to give more serious consideration to the British offer. He prepared a proposal that a Zionist commission be sent to East Africa to investigate the matter further.

The proposal was submitted to the Sixth Zionist Congress, held in Basel in August 1903. Though Herzl made it clear in his opening address that he had in no way abandoned his efforts on behalf of the establishment of a Jewish state in Palestine—and only in Palestine—and that what he proposed was merely a temporary expedient until arrangements were completed for such a state, he was assailed with anger and derision. A number of Russian delegates were especially upset; they believed that they had been betrayed by their leader's willingness to compromise in his effort to obtain the Holy Land as the homeland.

In the impassioned debate that followed, Herzl was angrily vilified as a traitor and a criminal by the opposition. It took all his diplomatic skills to convince many of the delegates that he was not asking them to choose between

East Africa and Palestine but merely to allow the congress to go ahead with an investigation of what he assured them would be only a temporary measure.

The issue threatened to disrupt the meeting and split the World Zionist Organization, but Herzl prevailed, and his proposal was finally accepted. Still, his margin of victory was so narrow, and the opposition so acrimonious, that the matter was dropped. Nonetheless, he had managed to save the organization he had founded.

By the end of the congress, Herzl was exhausted. The years of constant struggle and stress had taken their toll on him. His spirit seemed broken, and his health, which had troubled him sporadically for years, was deteriorating

Theodor Herzl (*with beard, seated at the table*) and journalists at the Sixth Zionist Congress, August 1903

steadily. A good friend remembered later that "the imposing figure was now stooped, the face was sallow, the eyes, those mirrors of a fine soul, were darkened, the mouth was drawn in pain. . . ." In the spring of 1904 he suffered a mild heart attack, and in early June he left for the Austrian mountain resort of Edlach to recover. He died there on July 3 of another heart attack. He was only forty-four years old.

His funeral took place on July 7 in Vienna. Mourners, who came from every corner of Europe, followed the hearse from the house in which he had lived to the cemetery. In his memoirs the journalist, historian, and man of letters Stefan Zweig wrote:

> The man being laid to rest was the leader of a great movement. . . . Vienna was suddenly being made aware that he was not just a writer or mediocre poet who had passed away but one of those creators of ideas who emerge only at the rarest moments in the history of countries and peoples. At the cemetery there was a mob scene. The crowds were pressing in on the coffin, weeping, howling, screaming in a wild eruption of despair that turned into a near-riot. All semblance of order broke down, swamped by a din of elemental and ecstatic mourning such as I have never seen before or since at a funeral. And this immense pain rising out of the depths of an entire people made me realize for the first time how much passion and hope this singular and lonely man had given to the world by the power of his ideas.

Herzl was, in the words of the great French statesman Georges Clemenceau "a man of genius, not to be confused with a man of talent. There was a breath of eternity in that man."

CHAPTER 2

CHAIM WEIZMANN

Born in Motol, Russia, on November 27, 1874
Died in Rehovot, Israel, on November 9, 1952
Married Vera Khatzman in 1906
Son Benjamin born in 1907
Son Michael born in 1916

CHAIM WEIZMANN

"To be a Zionist it is not necessary to be mad, but it helps."

Shortly after Herzl's death, Chaim Weizmann, a twenty-nine-year-old scientist and an ardent Zionist on his way to becoming another crucial figure in the history of Zionism, wrote to his future bride, Vera:

"I have had to experience a heavy blow. . . . At this moment, all the differences between us"—he and Herzl had often disagreed, most recently on the East Africa scheme—"have disappeared, and I have only the image of a great creative worker in front of my eyes. I feel a great weight on my heart and deep grief. He has left us a frightening legacy. Verochka, put on mourning. We are all wearing it. . . . Difficult times await me now. I feel that a heavy burden has fallen on my shoulders, and the shoulders are weak and tired. . . .

"I have one consolation: we are Jews, our destiny is different from that of any other people, we are a chosen nation, chosen in suffering, in torment, in feeling, and in our momentary but deep joys. I feel that some sort of ascetic attitude to life has begun developing in me, and I am afraid of it. We ourselves, and our personal future, do not frighten me in the least, and I am certain that everything will work itself out. But the general situation is getting worse and worse. . . ."

Chaim Weizmann and Theodor Herzl were in very many ways exact opposites. They differed radically in background, upbringing, education, interests, and personality. But they shared one goal, to which each passionately dedicated his life: the reestablishment of a homeland for the Jewish people in Palestine.

Weizmann was born on November 27, 1874, in a wooden house in Motol, a small village in the Pale of Settlement, a vast area in western Russia within which the czars had confined most of their Jewish subjects since the end of the eighteenth century. Between four and five hundred Russian and fewer than two hundred Jewish families lived in Motol. There was little contact with the outside world. Newspapers were almost unknown there. No railroad passed within twenty miles of the town, and there was no post office. In his autobiography Weizmann wrote: "But letters played no very important part in our lives; there were few in the outside world who had reason to communicate with us."

Chaim, the third of fifteen children of Ozer and Rachel Weizmann, was brought up in a warm and loving household. Theirs was among the most comfortable families in town. Though far from wealthy, they did have their own house, some acres of land, chickens, two cows, a vegetable garden, and a few fruit trees.

Ozer was a quiet, enlightened man with a passion for education and reading. The only Jew ever chosen to be the head of Motol, he was a diligent worker who earned enough money to support his large family by cutting hauling timber that was floated to the port city of Danzig, four hundred and fifty miles away. Rachel, according to Chaim, was not much of a housekeeper—with so many children to raise, she didn't have enough time—"but she was wonderfully good, the kind of person to whom neighbors turn naturally in time of trouble." Chaim remembered his mother as always "either pregnant or nursing an infant."

Judaism played a key role in the lives of the Weizmanns. Each member of the large family was devout and observant, none more so than Chaim. The young boy's education was largely traditional, beginning at four with daylong attendance at the nearby *cheder* (Jewish school), where the children studied the Talmud and the Bible. Chaim was fortunate, however. His education, unlike that of most of the other students, was not strictly limited to religious studies. One of his more enlightened teachers managed to smuggle into class secular Hebrew textbooks from which he allowed Chaim to read and thereby gain some knowledge of such nonreligious subjects as the natural sciences and chemistry. The boy was fortunate, too, that he was his mother's favorite and was treated as such.

In the early fall of 1885, shortly before Chaim's eleventh birthday, Ozer decided to send him to a Russian school in Pinsk, a larger town twenty-five miles south of Motol. Chaim had been raised in a typical *shtetl*, one of a number of small isolated Eastern European Jewish communities, and had had little contact with the outside world. Ozer believed that Chaim had by that time exhibited such precocious intelligence and seriousness that he could benefit in many ways from such a move.

First of all, he would learn the Russian language. In Motol, Hebrew was the language of his school, and Yiddish the language of his home. Knowledge of another language would enable him to live and function among a non-Jewish population for the first time. Consequently, and most important, in

Pinsk he would be exposed to another world in which he would have a chance to develop and absorb new ideas and interests. From Motol to Pinsk was a distance of only a few miles of travel, he noted. But the distance in terms of intellectual displacement was "astronomical."

Pinsk was, when Chaim arrived there, an active and lively city of thirty thousand inhabitants, the great majority of whom were Jewish. There were paved streets, libraries, factories, and shops as well as the nonreligious high school he would attend.

He remained there for seven years—very important years in his development—at the end of which he was able to say, "Pinsk set the double pattern of my life; it gave me my first bent towards science, and it provided me with my first experiences in Zionism."

Though he developed an interest in science in Pinsk, he had been exposed to Zionist ideas before then. Growing up in Motol under the influence of his learned father, he had been steeped in the tradition of Judaism and with it the belief that the Jewish people must return to the land of Israel. But there was no formal Zionist organization as yet; there would not be any until Herzl's time. There were only a number of small organizations, brought together under the name of Hovevei Zion ("lovers of Zion"), which advocated the return of the Jews to Palestine.

Chaim had been so enthusiastic about these ideas that when he was only eleven, he had written a remarkably perceptive and well-informed letter about "Jerusalem, which is our native land" to his teacher in Motol. Referring to the Hovevei Zion, he wrote:

> Through it we can save our downtrodden and despondent breth-
> ren who are scattered in all corners of the world and have no place
> in which to pitch their tents. We are being persecuted everywhere

and the Jew is a burden on all people. . . . The obligation lies upon us to find some place of refuge. Because even in America where knowledge prevails, and in all the countries of Africa . . . they will persecute us and have no mercy upon us. So let us carry our banner to Zion. Let us return to our first mother, on whose knees we were born. For why should we expect compassion from the kings of Europe, that they should, in their pity for us, give us a resting place? In vain . . . all have decided that the Jew is doomed to death but England will nevertheless have mercy upon us . . . let us turn to Zion! Jews, to Zion let us go . . . !

That advocacy of a return to Palestine developed into a passion for the young boy. Pinsk was a center of Jewish learning and culture and a focal point of Hovevei Zion activities, and he enthusiastically joined in heated discussions and debates both in his school and out of it. His interest in science also increased, largely the result of his contact with an excellent teacher who stimulated his interest in chemistry. "I have often wondered what would have been the course of my life it it had not been for the intervention of this gifted and fine-spirited teacher," he wrote.

His years in Pinsk (which he concluded was "just an enormous garbage heap,") had been, nonetheless, a formative and significant period for Chaim. But when he started planning for his university education after his high-school graduation, in 1892, he had to face the fact that he would have to leave not only Pinsk but czarist Russia in order to continue his studies. He had no regrets. Life was made extremely difficult for Russian Jewish students seeking a higher education; a very small percentage of those who applied to Russian universities were admitted, and consequently many thousands of them made their way to the West.

Chaim's first experience away from Russia was not successful. Following the example of two boys from Motol who left because they had failed to gain admission to the Pinsk high school, he traveled to the small town of Pfungstadt in southwestern Germany, where he found work as an assistant teacher of Russian and Hebrew in a Jewish boarding school. The money he earned enabled him to take courses in chemistry at the polytechnic in nearby Darmstadt. Although it seemed like an ideal arrangement, it was far from that. His classes bored him, and he found it impossible to make good friends. Unhappy, lonely, and exhausted (his workday began at five in the morning and ended late at night), he returned to Motol at the end of the academic year. He remembered Pfungstadt "without pleasure."

After spending an extended period at his parents' home, enjoying his mother's cooking and the warmth of his family's home life, he recovered sufficiently to return to Germany with far more successful results. This time he enrolled in one of Europe's finest scientific schools, the Charlottenburg Polytechnic near Berlin. Its chemistry department was excellent, and he was immediately recognized as an extraordinarily promising student. His activities outside the university were equally gratifying. Berlin, the capital of Germany, was a large and bustling city that attracted students from all over Europe. Prominent among them was a large colony of Russian Jews with whom the young man from Motol formed friendships and enjoyed debating Zionism, Palestine, and other stimulating controversial Jewish issues. Weizmann remained in the German capital for four years. They were a pivotal time, and he remembered that it was in Berlin that he grew out of the "boyhood Zionism" of his adolescence and into "something like maturity."

It was with mixed feelings that Weizmann left Berlin in 1898 in order to complete his formal education in Fribourg, Switzerland. His favorite professor from Berlin had moved to the Swiss university and urged his talented student to follow him. Weizmann earned his PhD there in 1899; the subject of his thesis was chemical reactions to dyestuffs, an interest that developed and served him well later in his life.

"When I left Berlin for Switzerland, at the age of twenty-four," Weizmann wrote years later, "the adult pattern of my life was set . . . [and] my life's purpose was crystallized." Certainly his two major interests—science and Zionism—had intensified and would occupy him for most of his life. These interests occasionally competed for his time and his attention, but the achievements of this brilliant man as both a scientist and a Zionist were remarkable.

Soon after his graduation from the University of Fribourg, it became clear that he was already far more than just a promising student of chemistry. His first scientific papers were published as early as 1899, when he was only twenty-five; in the same year he was appointed both a lecturer at the highly esteemed University of Geneva and assistant to a distinguished member of its chemistry department. Word spread that he was on the verge of a major discovery, a process that would substantially reduce the cost of a material basic to the manufacture of dyestuffs.

At the same time that he was making headway as a scientist, Weizmann was becoming increasingly committed to Zionism. Having participated in the many discussions among the Russian Jewish expatriate students who had flocked to Berlin and later to Geneva, he formed friendships with some of the most prominent Russian and German Zionists. Through these contacts, Weizmann, ever more passionately dedicated to the Zionist cause, revealed himself to be a skillful political strategist, one who possessed all the qualities necessary to assume, at some time in the not-too-distant future, leadership of the growing movement.

And the movement was spreading rapidly throughout Europe. The publication and subsequent fame, in 1896, of Herzl's *The Jewish State* gave it great impetus. Weizmann, though not much impressed by the book's contents (he found little that was new) was nevertheless encouraged by the emergence of a powerful, effective Zionist leader. He was even more enthusiastic about Herzl's call for a Zionist congress in 1897, and he urged his friends and colleagues to attend and present their ideas to the history-making gathering. Ironically, though he had been elected a permanent delegate from Pinsk—to serve for as long as these official Zionist conventions were held—he was, for personal and financial reasons, unable to be present. "I had the doleful satisfaction of learning," he wrote, "that I had been missed . . . my work in the movement was beginning to be known."

It was, as a consequence, not until the Second Zionist Congress, in 1898, that Weizmann had the opportunity to see Herzl. He was not overwhelmed by the Zionist leader:

62

> Though he was impressive, I cannot pretend that I was swept off my feet. There was a genuine greatness about him and a touch of pathos. It seemed to me almost at the beginning that he was undertaking a task of tremendous magnitude without adequate preparation. He had great gifts and he had connections. But these did not suffice. As I learned to know him better at succeeding congresses, my respect for him was confirmed and deepened. As a person he was both powerful and naive. He was powerful in his belief that he was being called by destiny to this piece of work. He was naive, as we already suspected from *The Jewish State* and we definitely learned from our contact with his work, in his schematic approach to Zionism.

Weizmann's approach to the creation of a Jewish state was different from that of Herzl, who believed that the Zionists' goal could be achieved only by means of diplomacy—through appeals to powerful statesmen and politicians and the wealthy ruling classes. Herzl believed those people were in the best position to guarantee, by legal and political means, the security of Jewish settlers in Palestine. He even believed that much of the money raised for the benefit of the new settlements should be held in trust until such guarantees were put into place and all investments in Palestine would be safe.

Weizmann disagreed with Herzl's dependence on diplomatic and political action as a means of achieving their goals. He and his followers criticized Herzl's aristocratic behavior, which was initially meant to appeal to the wealthy and powerful but in time also attracted the masses. Accusing him of being an elitist, they asked for a broader-based membership and support of the Zionist organizations. Most important, they called for immediate plans to strengthen the Jewish presence in Palestine, even before that presence was legally sanctioned. This meant developing a practical program of educational, social, and political activities so that the new settlers would be prepared for the time when their place in Palestine would be legally secured.

Weizmann did not hesitate to take sides in this conflict. In 1901, in Geneva, he had been prominent among a group of young delegates to the Zionist Congress who actively and energetically supported the views of those who opposed Herzl's policies. He joined them in establishing what was to be known as the Democratic Faction and soon became one of its leaders, urging the adoption of Hebrew cultural activities as a function of the World Zionist Organization and pressing for a larger measure of democracy in the leadership of the movement. When he and the other members of the group entered the meeting hall of the Fifth Zionist Congress at Basel at the end of 1901, they signaled the birth of the first Zionist opposition party, proof that the

63

WZO was no longer unified. And Chaim Weizmann, at the age of twenty-six, showed greater promise than ever of one day becoming the leader of the Jewish people.

The relationship between Weizmann and Herzl, never very close, reached a low point following the Sixth Zionist Congress and the bitter debate over the East Africa scheme. In a short and rather condescending note to the younger man, written even before the congress convened, Herzl had said: "I regard you, Dr. Weizmann, as a person who has been temporarily misled, but nevertheless as a useful force who will once more find his way back and proceed along the right road together with all of us."

The differences between them were based no longer just on strategy, but now on the very reason for Zionism's existence. Herzl believed that the major goal should be the establishment of a homeland where Jews could be safe, whereas Weizmann believed that the Jews must *return* to the ancient land of Israel.

Weizmann did not "find his way back." Instead he vigorously opposed those who supported, even as a possibility, the scheme to settle the Jews in East Africa, calling that support "a symptom of a sickness I have warned against for years." In a letter written following the congress to a Russian Zionist, he also expressed his concern and alarm over the problems that the Zionist movement was facing. "The present crisis was inevitable," he said. "It is the result of the abnormal position of the Jews. One group conceives of Zionism as a mechanism, and it is ignorant of its connection with the soul of the Jewish people. Consequently, it seeks to 'manufacture' Zionism either through diplomatic journeys or through fund-raising appeals. Elements that are partly detached from living Judaism—the assimilated Westerners on the one side, and the Orthodox confined within their rigid formulae on the other—are incapable of a better understanding of the national cause."

Weizmann was about to leave Geneva, where he had spent four years, when he learned of Herzl's death. He was profoundly saddened by the news. The two had had many angry disagreements, but Weizmann always remembered Herzl with great esteem and respect as a pivotal figure in the history of the Jewish people. He recognized Herzl's "magnificent gifts and complete devotion." Herzl was and remained for Weizmann "the classical figure in Zionism."

The Geneva years had been difficult for Weizmann. He had struggled, with mixed results, to strike a balance between his work as a scientist and his growing responsibilities as a leader of the Zionist movement. His academic duties at the University of Geneva, where he pursued his work in the organic chemistry laboratory under the supervision of Karl Graebe, a world-renowned chemist, were demanding, but he saw to it that most of his time went into his activities as a leader of the Democratic Faction. In this latter capacity, he set up an office in Geneva, from which he directed the affairs of the growing dissident Zionist organization. His primary responsibility was to insert Jewish cultural matters into the daily life of the Jewish people, and his achievements included the founding of a Jewish publishing house. His greatest passion was reserved for his efforts to establish the world's first Jewish university (in Palestine or outside it). The founding of such a university seemed to him urgent since Jewish students in Russia, elsewhere in Eastern Europe, and, increasingly, in Western Europe were widely discriminated against, making it almost impossible for them to gain entrance to institutions of higher education in their own countries. To be truly independent, the Jewish nation needed its own university, but its establishment required time and patience.

In spite of the time that Weizmann put into all his activities while in Geneva, he felt increasingly frustrated. It seemed that he had made little progress, not only in furthering the goals of the Zionist movement (he had found little support or enthusiasm for his dream of founding a Jewish university) but also in advancing his career as a scientist, which had stalled after his distinguished mentor had left the university. Geneva was an exciting, stimulating city, and he enjoyed the lively company and the ideas of the many students who had come there from all over the world, but he concluded that there was no longer any place for him there. There were already far too many wide-eyed expatriates filling the city's cafés and meeting halls with their ideas and plans for the future. Switzerland had become too small for him.

The choice for his next destination was the densely populated and heavily industrialized city of Manchester, in northwestern England. On a visit to London in 1903, he had made contact with a number of prominent British chemists and shortly afterward had received an offer from William Perkin, a professor of chemistry who specialized in Weizmann's field at Manchester University. The offer to join Perkin as his assistant came at the right time and was far too enticing to reject. Weizmann had been an Anglophile since early childhood. He admired Britain's people, ideals, and history. Above all, it seemed to him it was the country that would be most welcoming to the Jewish people and most receptive to the ideals of Zionism, a place where Jews would be judged strictly on their merits and not on their religion or political beliefs. Furthermore, though not nearly as interesting a city as the great capital of London, Manchester was the center of a major dye industry and therefore had great commercial potential for a young chemist.

Though he looked forward eagerly to meeting a new challenge away from Switzerland, he did not believe his years in Geneva had been wasted. "All in all, they were happy years, in spite of the troubles that weighed on us," he remembered, "for it is not in the nature of youth to be unhappy for long stretches at a time, though, to be sure, I could hardly count myself as part of the youth by the time my Geneva period was ended. I left Russia for the West a boy of nineteen; I left Switzerland for England a man of thirty. The ways of my life were set; the instruments of my activities were forged."

Weizmann arrived in England on July 10, 1904. After a few weeks in London, he moved on to Manchester. It was the beginning of a fruitful decade for him and for the Zionist movement.

The young man's admiration for Britain was certainly an important factor in his decision to settle there, but even more important was his belief that England—and specifically Manchester, with its university's excellent chemistry laboratory—offered him a unique opportunity to further his career as a scientist, which he feared was being neglected because of his passion for Zionism. He had been trained as a chemist and had no intention of abandoning his profession; he continued to find it fascinating as well as a potential— and occasionally essential—source of a good income. He was even willing to put aside his Zionist activities temporarily.

Because of his almost uncanny capacity to learn and assimilate knowledge rapidly, this latter step was hardly necessary. During his first months in Manchester he felt lonely and depressed. He had no friends—and only a few acquaintances, and making his way both socially and professionally was especially difficult because he was unable to speak or understand English fluently. He soon overcame this problem as his English rapidly improved, enabling him not only to make new friends but also to gain the respect and admiration of his colleagues at the university. (He was particularly proud that he was able to give his first lecture in English after only a few months of teaching.)

In Manchester, Weizmann's reputation as a teacher and as a research chemist grew; he published, in collaboration with other scientists, more than thirty papers and managed to find the time to work on a number of private research projects at a local dyestuffs factory. He did not, as he had initially feared, have to give up his political work. On the contrary, he was soon more involved in these activities than ever; an increasingly frequent participant at Zionist meetings throughout England and Scotland, he helped raise money and make policy decisions.

Most important, he was becoming well known, with a wide circle of friends and acquaintances, who were drawn to him because of his intelligence, ingratiating warmth, and wit. He was at home everywhere and welcomed wherever he went.

Having been born and brought up in a small Russian village, he traveled to and lived in the great cities of Western Europe, where he easily adjusted to other cultures. He was a scholarly man with a passion for education, who learned to speak and write English, French, and German while abroad as well as he had spoken Russian, Hebrew, and Yiddish in Russia. He was articulate, well informed, and persuasive as well as a born diplomat. He made contact and maintained social as well as political relationships with some of the most influential British statesmen and politicians of the time, who listened to him with respect and valued his opinions. His friend the British politician and writer Richard Crossman noted: "He always had the knack of being courteous without seeming obsequious and he was able to do this without play-acting, precisely because he always felt himself to be representing Jewry to a strange people whose help he needed and whose foibles he studied with a detached fascination." Weizmann was gradually becoming the spokesman best qualified to present the Zionist cause before a non-Jewish (as well as a Jewish) world.

While Weizmann was busy gathering support in Europe for the creation and eventual recognition of a Jewish state in Palestine, Jewish immigration to the Holy Land had been increasing. In spite of the often uttered wish "Next year in Jerusalem," relatively few Jews had gone to settle there in modern times. Most often they had done so in response to anti-Jewish decrees, such as the expulsion of the Jews from Spain in 1492, which left thousands of Jews homeless, or pogroms, which periodically forced them to seek refuge in other lands.

The first organized wave of Zionist immigration, which became known as the First Aliyah ("ascent"), began in 1882 (it lasted until 1903), when a small group of young Russians and Romanians, most of them students, reacted against the pogroms and persecutions that were sweeping across their own lands and made the long and arduous journey to Palestine in a desperate search for freedom and a homeland of their own. They were unprepared for what they found upon their arrival: a harsh, rocky, and arid terrain and a disease-ridden, undeveloped, and hostile land. Equipped with little more than the energy and idealism of youth, they understood the enormity of the hardships they would have to endure in their struggle to create a new land for themselves, but they were willing to make any sacrifices necessary in order to realize their dream.

Mere survival often seemed impossible. They, and the small groups of immigrants (usually young Russian intellectuals deprived of academic freedom at home) who followed them sporadically, had no funds to buy the equipment they needed—tools and plows—to cultivate and plant the barren land they encountered. Moreover, they had no money to purchase land from the Arabs on which to build new and more livable housing. They also lacked the skills to develop the land—they had no idea what to grow or when and where to grow it—or to construct the agricultural villages they envisioned. Furthermore, their hope that word of their effort would attract other young would-be settlers from Eastern Europe was frustrated by the ruling Turkish government, which issued orders restricting immigration and forbidding the sale of land to Russian Jews, many of whom were deported upon arrival. Although some twenty-five thousand Jewish immigrants entered Palestine between 1882 and 1903, even managing to organize the first Jewish agricultural settlements during that time, by 1904 only five thousand of these pioneers had survived the hardships and obstacles and were still living in these rural colonies.

From 1904 to 1914, during the next wave of immigration (or the Second Aliyah) thirty-five to forty thousand new Jewish immigrants entered Palestine. The large majority of those who had come before them had traveled there for ideological and religious reasons; theirs had been a homecoming, not an emigration. Many of the young pioneers who came later, on the other hand, were leaving their homes—presumably forever—to settle in a new land simply because they had no choice. The physical dangers of life in Russia and other Eastern European countries, characterized by pogroms and other anti-Semitic acts, had become unbearable, and the future was without hope for these young Jews. These idealists were more aware of the sacrifices they would have to make than their predecessors had been but were also determined to become the builders of a new Jewish nation—and on their own. Physical work, they believed, was sacred and essential to Jewish existence. The duty of the Jews was to make use of the land. This was their religion.

They soon realized that to achieve their ambitious goals, they would first have to master agricultural and construction skills. Until 1904, at the time of the beginning of the Second Aliyah, most of the workers in the new settlements had been Arabs who were far more experienced than the Jews and were willing to work for lower wages than these newcomers would. This dependence upon Arab labor, according to the new settlers, was no longer acceptable.

70

A Jewish nation had to be created by Jewish hands, not by the hands of non-Jews. It was nonsense, they believed, to maintain that Jews could not be laborers, that while they could be successful tailors or watchmakers or money-lenders, they were incapable of working in the fields or of building roads and houses and schools. These pioneers wanted to prove that the only reason they were not competent farmers or builders was that they had not been allowed to purchase the property that would have enabled them to practice these skills.

For this reason, a number of these settlers, who had been raised far from the farmlands, in the cities, towns, and villages of Eastern Europe, had to be trained as skilled workers. Then, and only then, could they concentrate on the other aspects—social, political, and cultural—that would also be essential elements in the building of a new Jewish society.

In a remarkably short time the pioneers set up a small training camp, which led to the creation and subsequent development of the unique collective agricultural settlement known as the kibbutz, the first of its kind not only in Palestine but in the world.

The establishment of the kibbutz was one of the most meaningful steps toward the development of the new nation. These inexperienced pioneers, financed and directed by agencies of the WZO, were given the opportunity to build on a small scale a new society based on their European socialist ideals and traditions. Without formally expressing their intention, they were in some ways following Weizmann's wishes that the foundations of the state be put into place before it was declared or legally recognized.

Another important step in the development of the new state was the building of a new city. It was to be called Tel Aviv ("hill of spring"), and in time it would become the new nation's cultural and commercial center.

Other endeavors followed. Most were in direct response to the needs of

The first kibbutz was called Degania ("cornflower" in Hebrew). It was located on a small piece of barren land on the east bank of the Jordan River that had been purchased from the Arabs with money raised by the Jewish National Fund. The initial purpose of this organization, founded in 1901 by the Fifth Zionist Congress, was to acquire, develop, and cultivate land in Palestine as national property, but its functions became so important and varied—every aspect of settlement and rebuilding was included— that a branch was opened in Palestine in 1908 to supervise its land purchases, most of them from absentee owners.

Degania and the many other social-ist collectives that were organized in the years to come proved to be more than just farm settlements; they became influential and frequently imitated experiments in human relations. The rules and charac-teristics varied in detail from kibbutz to kibbutz, but all adhered to the same principles of equality and social justice, which served as examples to the rest of the world.

Most important, there was no such thing as private property; everything was owned by the kibbutz. Individuals had no need for money. The collective supplied food, clothing, housing, and whatever else was required. Currency was never exchanged in the community, private trade was not permitted, and no outside labor could be hired. Marketing and purchasing were done by the group, not by any individual. All resources were pooled, and any profits were plowed back into the kibbutz.

There was little food, and what there was was of poor quality. In fact, life on every level was austere and ascetic, and the smallest show of extravagance or even comfort was looked down upon. The fam-ily as a unit was to be eliminated, and children were reared not by their parents but by all the members of the kibbutz. At first, it was even decided that the number of members of each kibbutz should be limited to twenty, so that the entire set-tlement might be considered an extended family, but in time this rule was often relaxed.

Kibbutz members cut fodder at Degania

Children in the Kibbutz Tel Yosef, early 1920s, Emer, Israel

TEL AVIV

In the spring of 1909 a group of young Jewish workers arrived at a windy stretch of land a few miles north of the largely Arab port of Jaffa. Equipped with shovels and trowels, they pitched their tents in the midst of twenty-seven acres of sand dunes near the sea and began to dig.

Their task was of historic importance. They were beginning the construction, on land recently acquired with the aid of the Jewish National Fund, of an entirely new city, Tel Aviv.

Because of the influx of Russian immigrants and the consequent over-crowding of Jaffa, where many of the immigrants settled, there was a pressing need for such a city in the first decade of the twentieth century. The plan was for a garden suburb outside Jaffa, a place where workers could relax after a day in the hectic city. Soon it became far more than that. It was a model of Jewish urban development in Palestine, designed by its founders down to the smallest detail. For

Founding of Tel Aviv, 1909

example, it was declared that "each property must have a garden, three meters wide, facing the street, and a fence."

The original plan had been to build sixty houses for sixty families. Instead, within five years—by 1914—Tel Aviv had become a flourishing city of 139 houses and a population of 1,500. It was on its way to becoming the first as well as the largest modern Jewish city in Palestine.

A family poses for a photo in the newly established town of Tel Aviv, 1909

the pioneers. One of them was, unfortunately, essential: the formation of a military defense force. Called the Hashomer ("watchmen"), it was founded in 1909 to defend the new villages against plunderers and, in later years, organized raids by potential enemies, who resented what they considered the intrusion of the settlers.

Other matters significant to the growth and development of the new society called for skillful efforts and long-term planning that were well beyond the needs of the kibbutzim. Hospitals and other medical facilities had to be constructed; an entire socioeconomic program organized and put into place. These included labor organizations, insurance companies, factories, railroad lines, and shipping services.

Understandably, Chaim Weizmann was not personally involved in any of these ventures. He was not a farmer, a builder, or a city planner. He was an inspired fund-raiser, a born leader who had a mission and a dream, the importance of which he was able to communicate expertly to audiences, small and large, wherever he traveled. His work could be most effectively done outside Palestine; in fact, he did not pay his first visit there until 1909, during the Second Aliyah, and that was a visit of only three weeks, during which he had been asked to investigate the possibility of establishing a chemical plant in the Holy Land.

One endeavor in which Weizmann's skills could be effectively used inside Palestine, however, was education. He was a man of the book, with a passion for the word, and he had since 1905 urged the adoption of a single common written and spoken language for all the Jews who came from many lands to live in the new state. Most of these immigrants spoke and read Yiddish, German, or even French, but a single language was needed to bind them together. The obvious choice was Hebrew, the language in which much of the Bible had been written and which had long been associated with the land of Palestine. It would have to be a modern Hebrew, not the language of the synagogues and the rabbis and the prayers, but a revised language in which the daily business of living and working could be conducted without offending the devout. Soon considered the official language of the Zionist movement and taught to Jews both in and outside Palestine, modern Hebrew spread rapidly. It quickly became the only language used in the settlements' nursery schools, elementary schools, and high schools. Before long it became the only language used in most educational institutions. Its popularity was extended by the publication of a Hebrew dictionary and the founding of Hebrew-language publishing houses, which issued newspapers, books of all kinds, and literary, political, and scientific periodicals.

Among the political, ideological, and educational Zionist leaders shown here are Chaim Weizmann, seated in the center, and to his left, Sir Herbert L. Samuel, first high commissioner of Palestine, 1918, in Yaffa

Weizmann also worked relentlessly for the establishment of a Hebrew university in Jerusalem, as he had for many years. Though his dream of what he had hoped would be one of the world's great centers of learning had not yet been realized, plans were going forward and land had been bought on Mount Scopus, one of the hills surrounding Jerusalem, to serve as the site of the university.

Weizmann's heart had been in this project since the Fifth Zionist Congress, when he backed a motion to investigate the possibilities for such a university. His enthusiasm increased when the idea was revived in the Eleventh Congress, in 1913, during which he busied himself with organizing and recruiting faculty members and with setting up a commission that resolved that immediate steps be taken toward creation of a university. It would first consist only of a medical school and departments of chemistry and physics and then develop into a full university. Weizmann's role in the university initially would be modest; he would be chairman of its chemistry department.

By 1914 there were approximately eighty-five thousand Jews in Palestine, some 12 percent of the total population. Immigration was increasing rapidly, and in the first six months of 1914 alone six thousand Jews came to settle there. The pioneers were building the foundations and framework of the new nation, and their dream of a nation of their own was, it seemed certain, on its way to becoming a reality. There was a feeling of energy, progress, and optimism in the air.

With the outbreak in the summer of 1914 of the World War and its spread throughout Europe and the Middle East over the next few years, all such optimism dissipated. Not only did the long and costly war throw doubts on the fate of the Jewish settlers in Palestine, but it also put into question the future of Palestine itself, torn between two powerful adversaries, the Ottoman Empire and Great Britain. Hopes of a Jewish nation faded as

Zionist immigration was suspended. Palestine became a dangerous destination for Jews, who were no longer wanted there. In early 1917 some twelve thousand Jewish settlers were evacuated from Tel Aviv and Jaffa by their Turkish rulers on the grounds that they were not Turkish citizens. Once again homeless, these and many other Jews of Palestine sought refuge elsewhere. Some were absorbed into Jewish settlements in the interior while others found asylum as far away as Egypt or Syria. Still others, those awaiting permission to immigrate to Palestine, were stranded homeless and desperate. Not until the war ended in 1918 were the Jewish settlers permitted to return to Palestine.

The countries engaged in the war made up a confusing tangle of shifting alliances and conflicting interests. The Ottoman Empire, of which Palestine had been a part since 1517, was leagued with Germany, Austria-Hungary, and Bulgaria against Great Britain, France, Russia, Italy, and eventually the United States. Unexpectedly, this controversial war (historians disagree on its causes and consequences) resulted in the greatest step to date toward the realization of the Zionist dream.

The man most responsible for this surprising by-product of the war was Chaim Weizmann. The years he spent in England preceding and during the war were highly productive. His reputation as a scientist grew in the classroom, where he inspired the many students who attended his courses, and in the laboratory, where the results of his experiments led him to numerous business and commercial applications, which in turn led to potentially lucrative patents. In that way he might even look forward to fortune as well as fame.

At the same time no matter how much of himself he put into his work as a scientist, he never lost sight of his goals as a Zionist. He traveled extensively, attended meetings, and lectured fervently on behalf of the establishment of a Jewish state at every opportunity. His was a commanding presence, and he made an indelible impression on those who met him or heard him lecture.

Most important, he was able to make friends and to mix comfortably with all strata—from high government officials to workers—of British society and to persuade many of the justice of the Zionist cause. (His position could only have been strengthened by the fact that he had become naturalized in 1910 and was therefore both Jewish and British.)

In 1914, with his exhausting schedule threatening to overwhelm him, Weizmann received what seemed to be an innocuous circular that changed the course of his life and that of the Jewish people. Sent by the British War Office, it requested that all scientists report any discoveries that might possibly aid the war effort. Weizmann replied at once, offering the War Office his fermentation process (then related to the production of badly needed synthetic rubber), which had occupied much of his time since 1910. He received no reply. Thinking that the data he had sent to the government were of no practical use, he continued his current, independent studies into the subject.

It apparently took two years to bring the potential importance of Weizmann's research to the attention of the War Office. Then, in March 1916, he was summoned to a meeting with the head of the British Admiralty's gunpowder department. The subject of the meeting was the acute shortage of acetone, a solvent that was essential to the manufacture of gunpowder and therefore a vital part of the British war effort. By the end of the meeting it was understood that Weizmann's fermentation process could, when adapted, be instrumental in the production of vast quantities of acetone. It was also decided that the scientist's own services to the government would then be indispensable. For a number of months he would have to divide his time between his university responsibilities in Manchester and his work for the Admiralty in London.

Weizmann soon realized that even he could not do justice to two demanding jobs at the same time, and by the middle of 1916 he had severed his connections with the university and moved to London. The transfer to the capital was highly successful. In Manchester, Weizmann had earned a solid reputation as a biochemist, but he had paid less attention to his responsibilities as a Zionist leader than he might have. This was not only because his obligations at the university took up so much of his time but also because in Manchester he did not have ready access to the governmental and political contacts that would be most useful to him in pursuit of his Zionist goals.

Once settled in London, Weizmann changed the focus of his activities. His achievements as a laboratory scientist were of broader significance than in Manchester, and they gained him additional respect and fame. He held a number of major positions, among them head of the British Admiralty laboratories, and he exercised his authority with tact and intelligence. Even more important, however, was the fact that through his government work he befriended some of the most illustrious people in British public life. With them he comfortably and skillfully assumed the role of a convincing propagandist for the Zionist cause. It was not a difficult role for him to play. He believed profoundly in the need for the Jewish national home, and he was able to express his passionate feelings in a lucid and convincing manner. He won a loyal following not only among the leading members of the Anglo-Jewish community but also among the leaders of the non-Jewish community.

The latter included some of England's most powerful political figures and statesmen, most of whom already supported the Zionist cause. One was Winston Churchill, first lord of the Admiralty, who had interviewed Weizmann and recommended him for his London position, and who was a firm believer in the need for a Jewish state. Another, C. P. Scott, editor of the *Manchester Guardian*, one of England's most widely read newspapers, who was known for his sympathy with Jewish ideals, put Weizmann in touch with the powerful British leader David Lloyd George, once the chancellor of

81

the exchequer, then minister of munitions, and, from 1916 to 1922, prime minister, who had long been a supporter of the Zionist cause.

Lloyd George was a devout Christian who believed that the establishment of a Jewish state was a prerequisite to the Second Coming (the return of Jesus as judge for the Last Judgment). So was Arthur James Balfour, the British statesman whose name is most closely associated with the Zionist cause. Balfour was a complex man. A strong-willed passionate student of the Bible, he had been torn between a career as a philosopher and that of a theologian (before choosing to become a statesman-politician) and had for a number of years been interested in Zionist objectives. Christianity owed the Jews "an immeasurable debt shamefully ill repaid," he once stated.

Weizmann had met Balfour in 1905, soon after Balfour had lost both the prime ministership (which he had held since 1902) and his parliamentary seat from Manchester. Weizmann tried to explain to Balfour why the East Africa offer, made during Balfour's tenure, was unacceptable. Toward the end of their meeting, which had been most cordial, Weizmann, according to his own version, said: "'Mr. Balfour, supposing I were to offer you Paris instead of London, would you take it?' He sat up, looked at me, and answered, 'But, Dr. Weizmann, we have London.' 'That is true,' I said. 'But we had Jerusalem when London was a marsh.'

"He leaned back," Weizmann reported, "continued to stare at me, and said something I remember vividly: 'Are there many Jews who think like you?' I answered: 'I believe I speak the mind of millions of Jews whom you will never see and who cannot speak for themselves, but with whom I could pave the streets of the country I come from.'"

When they met again some ten years later, Balfour, who had been first lord of the Admiralty in 1915 and later served as foreign secretary from 1916

The visit of Lord Balfour *(center in white suit)* to Tel Aviv on the occasion of the opening of the first agricultural laboratory. First from right is Meir Dizengoff, mayor of Tel Aviv, third from right is Chaim Weizmann.

to 1919, was even more interested in and enthusiastic about the Zionists' goals. "Mind you," the British statesman told Weizmann following their talk, "come again to see me. I am deeply moved and interested. It is not a dream, it is a great cause and I understand it. . . ."

Balfour encouraged and supported Weizmann whenever possible in the latter's pursuit of that cause. During his years in London, Weizmann had taken advantage of every opportunity to present the case for a Jewish homeland in Palestine under a British protectorate. He was in a strong position to do so. The warm relationships he had cultivated had been strengthened by the services he had performed for the Admiralty. He became known and admired as a man of unquestionable integrity. He was so highly esteemed that in July 1917 the government sent him as its representative on a secret mission to Gibraltar, to meet with the American diplomat Henry Morgenthau in an effort to foil American attempts to talk Turkey into making a separate peace with the Allies.

There were other signs that Weizmann and members of the British government could work together harmoniously. Since the beginning of the war, both Weizmann and Balfour had participated in government negotiations to prepare a pro-Zionist document that would pledge Britain's strong support for a national home for the Jewish people in Palestine. There were several reasons for such a statement. One was the British government's desire to take an idealistic position by declaring its solidarity with the harassed Jewish people. Another was that the declaration would gain essential wartime support from Jews in Europe and America. Finally, such an avowal would promote Britain's own strategic and territorial interests in the Middle East.

By early 1917 it seemed clear that the time had come to issue the statement. At the end of the previous year the strongly pro-Zionist Lloyd George had been named prime minister, and he was bringing into the government men of ideas similar to his own, creating the proper climate for such a move. For some time the war had been stalemated, but by 1917 the British appeared to be emerging victorious in Palestine and were preparing to capture it from a defeated Ottoman Empire.

In the late summer of that year Weizmann, having obtained the support of key members of the American government and of the London press, was convinced that it was urgent for the British government to make public its commitment to Zionism. On November 2, Lord Balfour wrote the following letter, addressing it (at Weizmann's suggestion) to Lord Lionel Walter Rothschild, president of the British Zionist Federation:

> I have much pleasure in conveying to you, on behalf of His Majesty's Government, the following declaration of sympathy with Jewish Zionist aspirations which has been submitted to, and approved by, the Cabinet.
>
> "His Majesty's Government view with favour the establishment in Palestine of a national home for the Jewish people, and will use their best endeavours to facilitate the achievement of this object, it being clearly understood that nothing shall be done which may prejudice the civil and religious rights of existing non-Jewish communities in Palestine, or the rights and political status enjoyed by Jews in any other country."

When Weizmann saw the completed document, he was disappointed. There were, he believed, significant omissions: no firm promise of a Jewish state and no mention of a British commitment to administer Palestine. Also, the language was often vague and ambiguous, not phrased exactly the way he had hoped it would be. Still, he recognized it as an achievement of historic importance. It was a turning point in Jewish history, a time for rejoicing. The Balfour Declaration, as it came to be known, represented the first public political recognition of Zionist aims by a major power. It is fair to say that without Weizmann's dedication, personality, and extraordinary diplomatic skills, there would have been no such declaration and no state of Israel. "One man's personality changed the course of history," according to Richard Crossman.

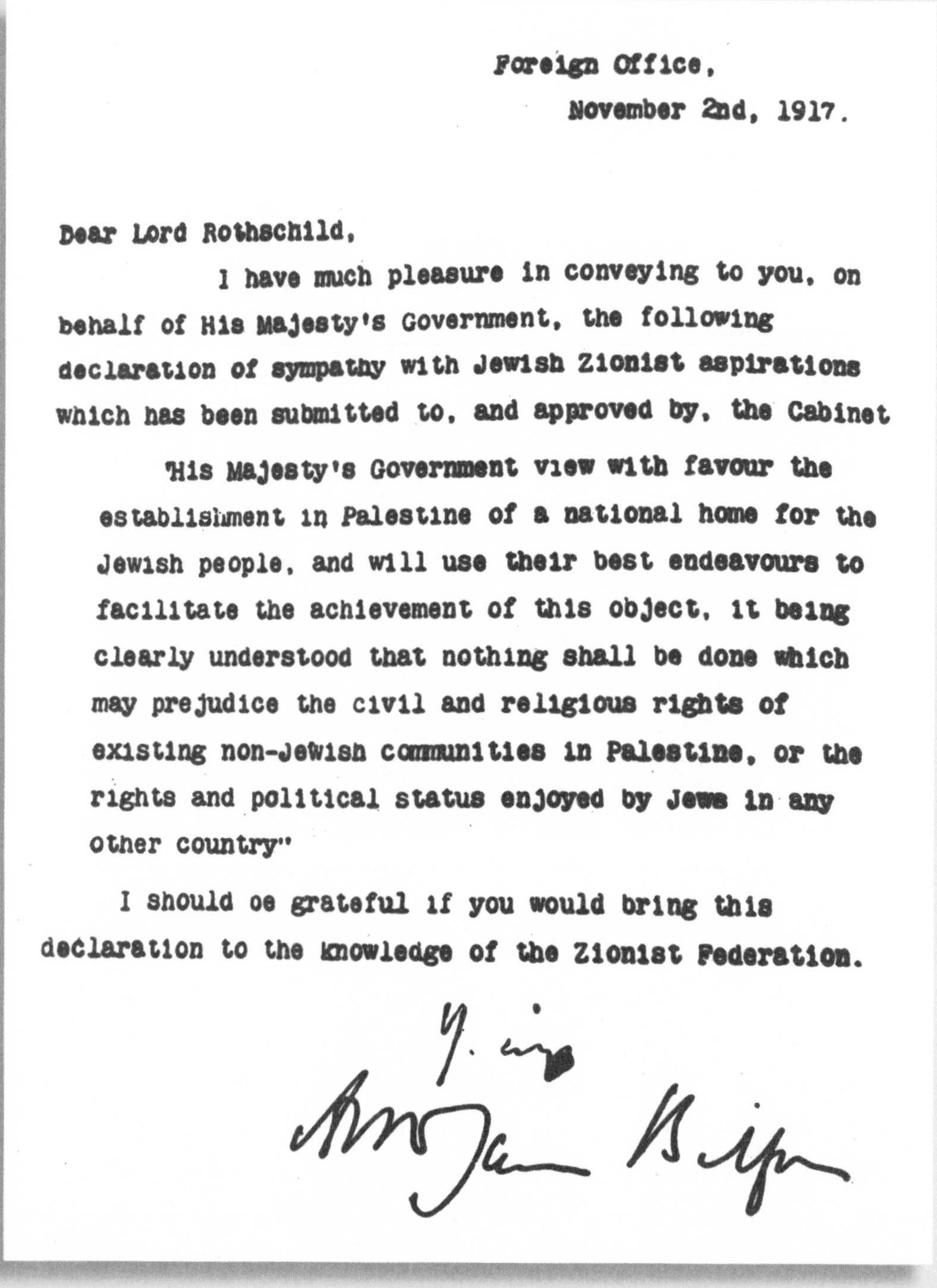

Foreign Office,
November 2nd, 1917.

Dear Lord Rothschild,

I have much pleasure in conveying to you, on behalf of His Majesty's Government, the following declaration of sympathy with Jewish Zionist aspirations which has been submitted to, and approved by, the Cabinet

'His Majesty's Government view with favour the establishment in Palestine of a national home for the Jewish people, and will use their best endeavours to facilitate the achievement of this object, it being clearly understood that nothing shall be done which may prejudice the civil and religious rights of existing non-Jewish communities in Palestine, or the rights and political status enjoyed by Jews in any other country"

I should oe grateful if you would bring this declaration to the knowledge of the Zionist Federation.

Y. ing

Arthur James Balfour

The Balfour Declaration

The reaction of Jewish communities throughout the world to the Balfour Declaration was predictably ecstatic. It actually seemed possible that the Jewish people could be on the path to a secure Palestinian homeland of their own. "A new chapter had been opened for us," Chaim Weizmann wrote in his autobiography, "full of new difficulties, but not without its great moments."

Weizmann was correct; there were many encouraging moments and many discouraging ones. The period immediately following the issuance of the declaration was filled with hope. In early December 1917 little more than one month after the Balfour Declaration, the British forces led by General Sir Edmund Allenby captured Jerusalem, and the general himself marched into the city to address a gathering of Muslims, Christians, and Jews on the steps of the historic Tower of David. His words set the tone for what he hoped would be the peace to come. "We have come not as conquerors but as deliverers," he proclaimed. "It is our intention to open a new era of brotherhood and peace in the Holy Land." The following September, Allenby, whose forces had been prevented from completing their conquest, first by winter rains and then by a bloody, prolonged last stand by Ottoman troops, began the last British action in Palestine. On October 30, 1918, Turkey signed an armistice, and on November 4 an armistice was concluded with Austria-Hungary. The same day a final Allied offensive was launched on the western front.

Sir Edmund Allenby

The end of the war was at hand. The German armistice was signed on November 11, 1918, and a peace conference to settle the boundaries of postwar Europe opened in Paris ten weeks later. On June 28, 1919, the Treaty of Versailles, the peace treaty with Germany that ended the war, was signed.

The future for a Jewish state in Palestine seemed bright. On April 25, 1920, Great Britain was granted the mandate for Palestine (the right to administer the territory until it was prepared to administer itself) by the members of the Supreme Council of the Paris Peace Conference. At a meeting of the council, held in San Remo, Italy, it was decided that the Balfour Declaration should be part of the mandatory statement. "Now you have got your start," Lloyd George told Weizmann, "it all depends on you."

Peace had returned, but the fate of the Jewish people—and their dream of a homeland—following the Balfour Declaration were still uncertain. Weizmann was among those who urged caution, asserting that a Jewish state was not automatically assured by the issuance of the declaration. A great deal of practical work still had to be done, he warned. After four hundred years under Ottoman rule in Palestine, they began three more decades there—this time, under a British administration. The mandate years, as they were called, opened with optimism but ended in anger, frustration, and disillusion.

There were many signs of progress toward the establishment of a Jewish national home. A new country was carefully being built by a determined and resourceful people who approached their task with courage and intelligent preparation. A legal system, based on Anglo-Saxon law but without a jury system and staffed by British magistrates, was put in place, as were improved and efficient postal, railway, telephone, and health facilities. Social reforms were instituted, and measures to encourage economic progress were undertaken. Innovative scientific methods were applied toward the solution of complex technical problems. Education, of course, was not neglected. One of Weizmann's most cherished dreams came true in 1925, when the Hebrew University of Jerusalem, which later became the largest institute of higher learning in the land, was formally opened at a deeply moving ceremony, held before an audience of twelve thousand on Mount Scopus and attended by both Weizmann and Lord Balfour, the latter, with tears in his eyes, resplendent in a scarlet gown.

Lord Balfour speaks at the opening ceremony for the Hebrew University of Jerusalem, 1925

CHAPTER 3

DAVID BEN~GURION

Born in Plonsk, Poland (then Russia), on October 10, 1886
Died in Tel Aviv, Israel, on December 1, 1973
Married Pauline (Paula) Munweiss in 1917
Daughter Geula born in 1919
Son, Amos, born in 1922
Daughter Renana born in 1925

DAVID BEN-GURION

"You can't be a realist if you don't believe in miracles."

Toward the end of the 1920s Chaim Weizmann's influence began to wane largely because his vision and temperament were not suited to the task of developing a group of struggling settlers into an organized, unified state. Fortunately there was a man, David Ben-Gurion, who was able to accomplish this complex and daunting mission.

David was born on October 10, 1886, the sixth child of Sheindel and Avigdor Green (the boy later changed his name to Ben-Gurion). Two of his siblings died before he was born, and four others died after, while a sister survived to adulthood. His mother, who died when David was ten years old, was warm and hospitable, while his father was formal and rigid. Tall and dignified, he was known as one of the most elegant men in town. David's childhood was in some ways similar to that of Weizmann. Like the latter, he was raised and went to school in a small impoverished town, Plonsk, in Poland (then Russia). He too was thoroughly steeped in Judaism although he was not religious and rarely attended synagogue after his bar mitzvah. At the age of three David learned Hebrew (actually on his brilliant grandfather's knee) and listened enthralled as his grandfather told stories of Jewish history, stories that made him realize that he was living among strangers in Plonsk and must eventually go to the land of Israel.

In this, the two youngsters differed, for David's father was a passionate Zionist who revered Theodor Herzl for his role in fighting for the cause of an independent Jewish homeland and passed his feelings on to his young son. As a result, David never forgot the excitement he felt when he heard a rumor, spread when he was ten years old (in 1896), that the Messiah had come and that he was a tall, handsome man with a black beard, a doctor named Herzl. . . .

Although he was astute and intellectually curious (his interests would later range from the Bible to Buddhism to the philosopher Spinoza) and an avid reader, young Ben-Gurion was not attracted to the academic world as was Weizmann. Nor did he resemble Weizmann physically. Energetic and dynamic, Ben-Gurion was short and slender with a disproportionately large head. His ambition was to fulfill Herzl's dream and realize the great leader's prophecy that a Jewish state would be created within fifty years. The new state would combine the ideals of socialism (he remembered *Uncle Tom's Cabin* and Avraham Mapu's *The Love of Zion*, two novels that dealt with injustices and racism, as being responsible for his becoming a socialist) with the concept of Jewish nationalism. He saw Zionism as a panacea for the problem of anti-Semitism and as a potential example for a just social order.

His Zionist activities began when, at the age of fourteen, he organized a number of his friends into the Ezra Society, a club whose aim was to transform Hebrew, generally used only in prayers, into an everyday language. This was a significant move, the beginning of his lifelong conviction that the Hebrew language must be the cultural tie that would hold together the

David Ben-Gurion *(third from right, front row)* and other members of the Ezra Society in Plonsk, Poland

new Zionist society. He loved languages and spoke Hebrew, Russian, Yiddish, German, Turkish, English, and a little Italian. He also learned to read Spanish in order to study Spinoza and Cervantes, but he never learned Polish, which he considered a "provincial" language.

A few years later, deeply disturbed by the increasing sense of estrangement he felt as a Jew in a non-Jewish world, he fulfilled what he saw to be his ultimate destiny as a Zionist: He abandoned his life and family in Europe and moved to Palestine.

He arrived in Jaffa on the morning of September 7, 1906. "My heart beat wildly," he wrote in his memoirs. "I had arrived." Once there, he felt himself reborn. He was a part of the Second Aliyah, the group of idealistic, energetic young men and women, committed to socialist ideals, who were bent upon laying the foundation for a workers' state in their new homeland. Like most of the young pioneers of the Second Aliyah, Ben-Gurion immediately sought work—as an agricultural worker in one of the small settlements—but jobs were scarce, and when available, they called for long days of hard labor under arduous and often unsanitary working (and living) conditions. This was difficult and even dangerous for a slight young man unused to hard physical labor. Inevitably, Ben-Gurion's health deteriorated, so much so that a physician cautioned that he could not long survive the attacks of malaria that he occasionally suffered. He considered malaria a badge of honor, and despite the dire warning, he stubbornly persisted. He firmly believed that Jews must make it their priority to return to the land and that settlement of the land was the only true Zionism. He had no intention of abandoning that land, no matter how hard the struggle.

Those first years in Palestine were intensely active for Ben-Gurion. They marked the gradual transformation of the relatively inexperienced, though doggedly determined, Zionist into an effective and increasingly influential leader. Exciting ideals were brought to fruition during those years; among them were the establishment of the first kibbutz and the founding of Tel Aviv. Though Ben-Gurion was not personally involved in these first two landmark achievements (he did not live in a kibbutz but lived, instead, in a new model agricultural camp at Sejera), he was instrumental in the creation of the military defense force Hashomer.

In 1910 the young man decided that he could make a more effective contri-

Hashomer movement members, Upper Galilee

bution to his new homeland by redirecting his energies from agricultural pioneer-
ing to politics, at which he was becoming increasingly adept. His first step was to
move to a major city, Jerusalem, where he hoped to find work as a journalist.

Jerusalem, when Ben-Gurion arrived, was a growing city. Many Jews had
moved there during the First Aliyah, and by 1890 there were some forty thousand inhabitants, more than half of them Jewish. The majority of these Jews

had lived on charity (funds collected in the Diaspora and distributed among needy pious Jews in Palestine) until the late 1880s, when the city began to change. Modern educational and medical institutions and enterprises were established. The population grew as the city modernized. By 1912 there were seventy-five thousand inhabitants, more than forty-eight thousand Jews, ten thousand Muslims, and nearly seventeen thousand Christians.

Soon after his arrival, Ben-Gurion found a job working for *Ha'Ahdut*, a new Hebrew socialist newspaper, which reflected his views and had become the voice of a young and vigorous socialist labor political party. He enjoyed his work, especially the chance to express his political views in the pages of a newspaper, but he was still not making full use of his extraordinary gifts as a politician, a diplomat, and a highly skilled organizer. He could find personal fulfillment and best serve the cause for which he was eager to devote his life only if he could spend all his energy and enthusiasm striving for the realization of his dream—the creation of a Jewish state in Palestine.

As a step in that direction he left his job and made a bold decision. Encouraged by the apparently successful fight for democratization being waged within the Ottoman Empire (which he believed would probably determine the future of the Jewish homeland), he decided that it would be more effective to work for the Jewish cause within the existing government. For that reason, he traveled with his friend Yitzchak Ben-Zvi (later the second president of Israel) to Constantinople, the capital, in 1912, to familiarize himself with Turkish laws and customs. After learning the Turkish language—in three months!—Ben-Gurion enrolled as a law student at the University of Constantinople with the aim of embarking upon a political career in Turkey following graduation. To function better within the Turkish social system, he even wore Turkish clothing.

Law students David Ben-Gurion *(left)* and Yitzchak Ben-Zvi in Turkey

His studies in Constantinople were interrupted by the world war. He hurriedly returned to Jerusalem, where he found masses of frightened Jews, uncertain of their future and fleeing, in panic, to Egypt. Despite the urging of his Jewish friends and colleagues (among them Chaim Weizmann) to back the British and the other Allies in their war against the Turks, Ben-Gurion continued his support of the Turks, trying to convince his fellow Jews to join him. At the same time, he helped expand the activities of the Hashomer into a general Jewish militia to defend all Palestine.

Ironically, only a short time later the Turks, suspecting that the Palestinian Jews (Ben-Gurion among them) might be secretly working for the British, arrested a large number of them and sent them out of Palestine. Ben-Gurion, one of the first to be arrested, sailed for New York in March 1915.

His arrival in the United States was energizing. "I always dreamed of America," he later wrote, "its vigorous, ultramodern life. . . . We who want to build a new country in the desert, to raise our ruins, we must see how exiles, persecuted in England, constructed a state so rich, with unequaled power."

He took full advantage of his time in America. Disillusioned by his experience under Ottoman rule, he now offered his wholehearted support to the British cause, recruiting American members for a Jewish Legion that was being organized as part of the Royal Army in London. Active within the Jewish labor movement in New York, he also led efforts to set up the Hechalutz ("pioneer") movement in America. This movement, while encouraging and facilitating the emigration of young American Zionists, offered them the same training that he had been given before moving to Palestine: instruction in military and agricultural skills as well as lessons in Hebrew.

Ben-Gurion's enthusiasm for the Zionist cause intensified during his time in America, particularly after November 1917, when the news of the Balfour Declaration seemed to indicate that the dream of a Jewish state might soon become a reality. He was overjoyed. "The greatest state in the world has announced its official recognition of the existence of a Hebrew nation, and has committed itself to aid in the establishment of a National Home in Palestine," he wrote. Although encouraged by the historic document, he recognized the continuing need for self-reliance on the part of the Jewish people. "Britain has made a magnificent gesture; she has recognized our existence as a nation and has acknowledged our right to the country," he wrote. "But only the Hebrew people can transform this right into tangible fact; only they, with body and soul, with their strength and capital, can build their National Home and bring about their national redemption."

In 1918 he returned to Palestine, then temporarily under British military rule. After years of social and economic disarray, most of the Jewish settlements were in bad condition and much of the work accomplished in the past had been destroyed. The young labor leader took charge. Again turning to politics, with more passion than ever, he rose rapidly to prominence and power in the thriving socialist labor movement. As the Jewish influx from Eastern Europe during the postwar period (the Third Aliyah) grew—to a rate of one thousand a month by 1920—his efforts to build a unified organization for the purpose of managing the affairs of the Palestinian Jews increased and resulted in the founding in 1920 of the Histadrut, or the General Confederation of Labor. The ambitious goal of this unique organization was to mobilize and unite all pioneers, farmers, and laborers for the good of the future Jewish state. The opening resolution of the first Histadrut conference expressed its goals by stating: "It is the aim of the United Federation of all the workers and laborers of Palestine who live by the sweat of their brows without exploiting the toil of others, to promote land settlement, to involve itself in all economic and cultural issues affecting labor in Palestine, and to build a Jewish workers' society there." Its slogan was: "We must make a nation of the class we represent."

Ben-Gurion was elected and served as the general secretary of the Histadrut from 1921 until 1935. He regarded his role within the organization as a potential power base for the realization of all his Zionist aims. Under his leadership, it became far more than an ordinary trade union. In time it was the dominating influence on the land's economy, an all-embracing political, social, and economic institution, with a network of factories, development corporations, health services, and financial institutions.

The Histadrut did not limit itself to improving the lot of its members. It provided social services for them, took over their hospital and sanitation

David Ben-Gurion speaks at the cornerstone-laying ceremony for the Histadrut building, Jerusalem

facilities, administered their welfare agencies, and supervised their schools. Furthermore, in order to increase employment opportunities for newly arrived immigrants, most of whom were excluded from British and Arab projects, it entered the construction business and contracted for public commissions. In these ways the Histadrut provided the economic infrastructure as well as the social fabric for the future state.

The Histadrut's power, under Ben-Gurion, expanded steadily. In 1929 he was instrumental in merging the two largest political socialist parties to form the Mapai party. He immediately folded it into the Histadrut, and in 1930 he allied the Mapai with other smaller socialist parties. Thus, the Histadrut, under the Mapai banner, gained political dominance as well. It remained dominant for some fifty years and marked the political direction that the new country followed in its early years.

During the decades of the British mandate Ben-Gurion emerged as the architect of the Jewish state as well as the leader of the Zionist movement. He was recognized as the man who built the new nation, brick by brick, skillfully and pragmatically, according to the broad, clear vision of Israel's destiny. Ben-Gurion's influence in the Zionist movement extended beyond the borders of Palestine. He represented Palestinian labor at international socialist gatherings in the 1920s and 1930s and spoke for it before committees that investigated Palestinian matters during those years.

He differed in many ways from the illustrious figures who had preceded him on the path to the Jewish state. He made no attempt to imitate Herzl's majestic, dignified bearing and appearance; the latter, a worldly Hungarian-born journalist and writer, who dressed meticulously to impress the public with the seriousness of his efforts, probably would not have approved of Ben-Gurion's open collar and rolled-up sleeves, which he wore to identify himself as one of the crowd. The labor leader from Plonsk differed from Weizmann, too. He lacked the latter's subtle humor and engaging, magnetic, worldly charm. The often modest and humble Ben-Gurion sometimes had difficulty in relating to strangers, while Weizmann easily made friends with people in every walk of life and in every part of the world.

Under Ben-Gurion's leadership, a great deal of progress was being made, but it was slow and far from steady. There were, as Weizmann had foreseen, many serious obstacles to be overcome. One stemmed from the fact that the wide and generous support that Great Britain offered the Zionist cause in 1917 had for the most part disappeared by the early 1920s. There had been many deceptions, contrary assertions, and broken promises on the part of the British concerning Palestine. Balfour himself wrote: "So far as Palestine is concerned, the Powers have made no statement of fact which is not admittedly wrong, and no declaration of policy which, at least in the letter, they have not always intended to violate." Another most serious obstacle was the increasingly hostile relationship between the Jews and their Arab neighbors.

Before the turn of the century, relations between Arabs and Jews could have been characterized as reasonably cordial, if not friendly. Most of the properties the new Jewish settlers purchased had belonged to a small group of wealthy Muslim families that controlled but did not live on the land. This land—a poorly cultivated, widely neglected expanse of sandy deserts, eroded hills, and disease-ridden marshes—was thinly populated and worked by tenant sharecroppers or fellahin.

In acquiring the land, the new immigrants displaced these desperately poor men and women, and often because of cultural misunderstandings, injustices were inevitably committed. On the other hand, the new immigrants hired Arab workers and bought Arab foods. Co-operation was not uncommon between members of the two groups, who were also on occasion guests in one another's homes.

With the increase in Jewish immigration and a rise in Arab nationalism—awareness of and pride in being a separate, unique people—during the first decade of the twentieth century, Arab resentment of the new settlements grew. By the end of the war, isolated, disorganized Arab attacks on these settlements had increased in number and efficacy, and by 1920 it was clear that the Arab leaders and their followers, encouraged by the viciously anti-Jewish mufti (Muslim religious leader) of Jerusalem, Haj Amin al-Husseini, saw Zionism as a serious danger.

Opposite page: An Arab farmers' market on the border between Jaffa and Tel Aviv, 1934

It was then that these random attacks grew into larger, well-planned, organized riots, meant to reduce the number of Jewish immigrants permitted to enter the country and to weaken (or abolish) the Balfour Declaration. In general, the Arabs' goal was to diminish the power and position of the Jewish settlers and frequently to gain a specific concession from the British for the Arab cause. The first of these disturbances took place in April 1920; its purpose was to influence the Allied representatives who were meeting in San Remo to dispose of the postwar mandates and to discuss whether or not to include the Balfour Declaration as a part of the mandatory statement. The riot began with attacks on a number of small Jewish settlements and culminated in a large demonstration in Jerusalem. The crowd was soon out of control, and violence ensued. In three hours some 160 Jews were injured. Finally, by nighttime, British troops arrived and put an end to the bloodshed (some observers thought the British did as much or more to hinder the Jewish defense as to help it). Whatever the case, the truce the British established was short-lived; fighting resumed the following morning and lasted for three days, during which a number of Jews and Arabs were killed and several hundred injured. The aftermath was almost as upsetting for the Jews as the bloodshed itself. Most of the Arab participants were given light prison sentences while the leaders of the Jewish defense were sentenced to fifteen years each.

These terrible riots did produce two positive results for the settlers. First, in June 1920, realizing that the British authorities could not be depended upon to protect them, a group of Jewish leaders, including Ben-Gurion, founded the Haganah, an underground defense force, completely free of foreign control, to safeguard their interests. This clandestine defense force proved to be of vital importance in the years of the British mandate.

Opposite page: Sir Herbert Samuel, British High Commissioner for Palestine from 1920 to 1925

דמיהנאציב העליון ברהבון

In addition, word of the injustices committed during and after these riots unleashed an unprecedented wave of sympathy for the Zionist cause. Protests and petitions arrived from all over the world. Among them was a cable from Woodrow Wilson, the American president, and his cabinet pledging their support of the Zionists' aspirations. The British public, too, responded sympathetically to the settlers' cause. Parliament was deluged with petitions, and the British press insisted that the government keep the promises it had made to the Jews.

On August 25, 1920, the Balfour Declaration was incorporated into the peace treaty, and Great Britain was officially made the mandatory for Palestine. As a result, there were more Arab disturbances.

The first took place in May 1921, when groups of Arabs, demanding the abolition of the Balfour Declaration, staged riots in Jaffa and the surrounding countryside that led to the deaths of forty-seven Jews and forty-eight Arabs, with several hundred on both sides injured. Shortly after British troops managed to stop the violence, an official commission of inquiry was established to determine the cause of the outbreaks. Its report was, from the Zionists' point of view, disturbingly pro-Arab. The most upsetting part was a call for a ban on Jewish immigration. The ban lasted only a few months, but the decree lifting it included strict limitations on Jewish immigration, including the guarantees of employment for the new immigrants.

Obviously, both the ban and the subsequent restrictions on immigration caused great apprehension among Palestinian Jews concerning the stability of what they hoped would be their permanent future homeland. On the other hand, the Zionists paid surprisingly little attention to the separation of the territory of Transjordan, to the east of the Jordan River, from Palestine. This was an admission of the fact that Transjordan, nominally within the boundaries of the mandate, would eventually be included not in Palestine but in a zone of Arab autonomy.

In June 1922, in order to summarize and clarify the British government's interpretation of the Balfour Declaration, an official document, to be known as the Churchill White Paper, was issued. (Official British government policy statements were called white papers; those concerning Palestine became known by the name of the incumbent colonial secretary—in this case, Winston Churchill—who did not necessarily write them.) While reaffirming the Balfour Declaration, the paper stated that the Zionists could not

High Commissioner Herbert Samuel *(left)* and British Colonial Secretary Winston Churchill in Jerusalem during the British mandate, 1921

contemplate transferring Palestine as a whole into a Jewish national home, that Palestine was not to become "as Jewish as England is English" but instead was to be "a center in which Jewish people as a whole may take, on grounds of religion and race, an interest and a pride." In order to assure the Arab community that Palestine would not be inundated by Jewish settlements, the White Paper, while confirming the right of Jews to immigrate to Palestine, stipulated that this immigration be based on the "economic absorptive capacity of the country."

Following the issuance of the White Paper, but not because of it, relations between Jews and Arabs seemed to improve, so much so that Weizmann, in 1924, believed that the Arab question "had lost a great deal of its acuteness." Emphasizing the need to get along, he wrote: "[W]e have told the Arabs, and we mean it, that we come to Palestine not as conquerors but as a people returning to its home. We shall not take from them any of their possessions, neither shall we take from them their language or their culture. We shall cooperate with them. We shall do everything to help them fructify the land from the Euphrates to the river of Egypt." He repeated this message in an address to the Zionist Congress in August 1925: "Palestine must be built up without disturbing a hair of the legitimate interests of the Arabs. The Zionist Congress must not confine itself to platonic formulae. It must recognize the fact that . . . 600,000 Arabs are there who, from the point of view of international justice, have just as much right to their life in Palestine as we have to our National Home."

Despite Weizmann's apparent optimism and his offers of mutual cooperation, hostility between Jews and Arabs had not disappeared or even diminished. It had merely been festering, and it burst out with unprecedented rage during the summer of 1929. In 1928 a relatively trivial dispute between Jews and Arabs was exploited by extremists on both sides and used for many months by the mufti of Jerusalem in an effort to inflame his people against

110

the Jewish population. Preceded by massive Jewish demonstrations in Tel Aviv and Jerusalem, the fierce rioting began on August 23, 1929, in Jerusalem. The looting and fighting soon spread throughout Palestine—to Jaffa, Haifa, and especially Hebron and Safed. Along the way six Jewish agricultural settlements were completely demolished. Because of ineffective police action, it was not until August 28 and the arrival of British troops that order was completely restored; by that time several hundred Jews and Arabs had been wounded or lost their lives.

These devastating riots gave proof of the deep-seated resentment that the Arab population continued to feel toward the Zionists and their proposed homeland. It also exposed the inadequacy of the British forces and the (perhaps inevitable) bias that the Arab police displayed in their behavior to their own people. In addition, it was evidence of the failure of the British pro-Zionist policy.

On the basis of official reports issued following the riots, it was becoming clear that the British government was no longer in sympathy with the Zionist cause. The first report was the result of a study made by a formal commission of inquiry, headed by Sir Walter Shaw, to ascertain the riots' causes and recommend measures to prevent their recurrence. The commission stayed in Palestine for three months, at the end of which time they concluded that the riots had not been planned by the mufti or the Arab leadership. While conceding that the Arabs should be held responsible for the bloodshed, the report stated that their anger was due only to their fears that Jewish immigration and land purchases would deprive them of their livelihoods and eventually turn them into a landless minority under the complete domination of the Jews. There had been, the commission found, too much uncontrolled immigration as well as too little compromise on both sides. As a result, Jewish immigration had to be limited, and Arab tenants protected from eviction because of Jewish land purchases.

The British government responded favorably to the report. It suspended thirty-three hundred recently issued Jewish labor certificates and announced that it would consider further measures to protect the Arab population. In addition, it sent Sir John Hope Simpson, an authority on agricultural economics, to Palestine to make recommendations concerning land settlement and immigration, among other matters. Hope Simpson's report, not surprisingly, reached the same conclusions that the Shaw Commission's had.

The Jews were enraged. Ben-Gurion, making his first appearance in the political role of Zionist diplomat, did his best to convince the British that they were mistaken. In the past Ben-Gurion's actions had been confined to the Histadrut and trade unionism; henceforth his political activities on behalf of the Zionist executive took up the better part of his skills and time.

Before there was a chance to lodge a formal protest, however, Britain issued an even more offensive report, the Passfield White Paper. Stressing that Great Britain's obligations to the Jews were no greater than its obligations to the Arabs, it called for the suspension of Jewish immigration as long as there was extensive unemployment in Palestine. In addition, it called for an end to further land purchases by noting that "there remains no margin of land available for agricultural settlement by the new immigrants, with the exception of such undeveloped lands as the various Jewish agencies hold in reserve." Without saying so in so many words, this latest White Paper was in effect a refutation of the Balfour Declaration.

The response to Lord Passfield's statement was immediate and indignant. There were angry protests not only from Jewish communities all over the world but also from members of Parliament. As a result, Passfield retreated, assuring Chaim Weizmann, who had led the protests, that the Zionists had misunderstood his White Paper. This was eventually followed by an official letter from Prime Minister Ramsay MacDonald to Weizmann, asserting that there had been no reversal of British policy and that the government had no intention of repudiating the Balfour Declaration or abandoning the terms of the mandate.

The Palestinian Jews were both relieved and emboldened by the prime minister's letter. It signaled the beginning of several years of few—and minor—clashes with their Arab neighbors, which consequently helped the Zionists make what Weizmann called the "magnificent gains" of the 1930s, gains toward transforming their land into the functioning prosperous state of the future. The signs were good. The economic situation, which had been poor, was improving, as was immigration. In 1933 alone, some thirty thousand settlers arrived, the highest number in any one year. The years 1933 to 1935 were years of unprecedented prosperity in Palestine.

Outside Palestine, however, the situation was not encouraging. Adolf Hitler seized power in Germany, where he made himself dictator and soon initiated a policy of vicious anti-Semitism, at first disenfranchising, then terrorizing, and finally killing the Jews of Germany and, in time, causing the annihilation of the Jewish communities of the many European countries he conquered. Furthermore, in the 1930s several Arab nations close to Palestine were granted varying degrees of independence, Iraq and Egypt by the British and Syria and Lebanon by the French, giving rise to a new feeling of Arab unity and nationalistic pride. This development also intensified the resolve of the rabidly anti-Zionist Arabs within Palestine to resume their assaults on the Jewish population. Now, with the support of their neighbors, they were able to attack Jewish settlements, engage in guerrilla warfare, and assail individual

Rail pass issued by the British giving the bearer permission to travel in Palestine at his own risk

Jews throughout Palestine with renewed strength. In a full-scale revolt, the Arabs turned on both the Jews and the British occupiers.

Finally, in November 1936, the British government sent a royal commission, under the chairmanship of Lord Robert Peel, a lawyer and distinguished colonial administrator, to Palestine. Its assignment was to make a detailed investigation of the cause of the disturbances, which had resulted in almost three thousand casualties (Arabs, Jews, and members of the mandatory) and to ascertain if either side had justifiable grievances. In addition, it was once again to make recommendations for an end to the complaints and prevention of their recurrence.

The commission remained in Palestine for more than two months and in the course of 66 meetings heard 113 witnesses. Chaim Weizmann came out of four years' retirement as a political leader—he had traveled on fundraising missions and worked on behalf of the future Weizmann Institute of Science—and he and Ben-Gurion were among the first to be heard. Both testified that in spite of the disturbances, Jews and Arabs could live together once an agreement was reached. Ben-Gurion asserted that the Zionists had no intention of making Palestine into a Jewish state. He was aware that there were non-Jewish inhabitants who did not want to be at the mercy of the Jews, just as the Jews did not want to be at their mercy. "A state may imply . . . domination of others, the domination by the Jewish majority of the minority," he said. That, he insisted, was not the aim of the Zionists. It had never been, nor would it ever be.

Weizmann too repeated that once a legislative council was established, the Jews would never claim more than an equal number, no matter what the ratio between the Arab and Jewish populations should be. The principle of parity would be maintained. According to him, the commission was "by far the most distinguished and ablest body ever sent out to Palestine." He was impressed by its proceedings.

The commission report, a four-hundred page volume, was issued in July 1937. The carefully detailed document was markedly sympathetic to the Zionist settlers. Jewish immigration, it noted, by supplying capital, manpower, initiative, and technical skill had benefited the entire population of Palestine, including the Arabs. Nonetheless, the commission concluded that there was no cure for the disease afflicting Palestine; the differences between Jewish and Arab interests were so deep-rooted and irreconcilable that the only hope was in a "surgical operation." This would mean the end of the mandate and the partition of Palestine into two separate states, Jewish and Arab, with a British-controlled corridor that would include Jerusalem.

This was a drastic solution to a very serious problem, but given the qualifications of the members of the commission, it was worthy of careful consideration by both sides. The Arabs rejected it immediately. They wanted an end to any idea of a Jewish national home as well as to all immigration and further land sales. Delegates to the Zionist Congress, which met in Zurich

Chaim Weizmann and David Ben-Gurion *(right)* meeting in Switzerland

in August 1937, moreover, were divided when the plan was presented to them. Many thought that it should be rejected on the grounds that the size of their state would be too small under the terms of the proposal. Others, led by Weizmann, while agreeing that the plan as conceived was unacceptable, believed compromise should be sought. After all, a compromise would mean that the dream of a Jewish state would become a reality far sooner than even the most optimistic Zionist had expected. After a long debate Weizmann convinced the delegates, including Ben-Gurion, who had initially been skeptical, that a state reduced in size was better than no state at all. Ben-Gurion was authorized to enter negotiations with the British government in the hope that the terms of the plan might be improved.

It was too late for that, however. In the summer of 1937 the Arab revolt resumed, and several hundred more Jews were killed. The British government, convinced that there could never be a solution to the problem without the agreement of the Arabs, sent another commission to Palestine. Its purpose was to study the feasibility of partitioning Palestine as recommended by the Peel Commission. Its conclusion was reached without the cooperation of the Arabs, who boycotted the meetings; their position was ably presented by British participants who were openly anti-Zionist. The commission found that the partition plan was unworkable and recommended other approaches.

One such approach was a conference that would bring together representatives of Arabs and Jews for a meeting with British leaders to discuss the future of Palestine. Opening in London in February 1939, the London Conference began badly when the Arab leaders refused to sit in the same room as Weizmann and the other Jewish representatives. In addition, they declared that they would not be party to any agreement that called for future Jewish immigration or land purchases. Perfunctory talks occurred, but after a few weeks the British, thoroughly disheartened, ended the conference, promising to work out a solution without suggestions from either the Jews or the Arabs.

That solution, issued in May 1939, was known as the MacDonald White Paper, named after the colonial secretary Malcolm MacDonald, son of the former prime minister. Calling for an end to all Jewish immigration after a period of five years, during which a maximum of seventy-five thousand Jews would be allowed to enter Palestine, it gave in to all of the Arabs' principal demands. This was not at all surprising since the British had already decided that it was far more in their interest to placate the Arabs, in an effort to stop them from siding with Britain's enemies, Germany and Italy, than to please the Jews, who could offer them little material or strategic support—or, for that matter, oil. However, it came as a tremendous shock to Weizmann, Ben-Gurion, and the rest of the

Zionist leaders, for it effectively withdrew British backing for a Jewish state by rescinding the principles of the Balfour Declaration.

On September 1, a few months after the issuance of this latest white paper, the Jews suffered another serious blow. The powerful troops of Hitler's Germany invaded Poland, signaling the beginning of World War II and marking a further step toward the destruction of European Jewry. Choosing sides between Great Britain, which the Jews believed had betrayed them, and Hitler's Germany, which wanted to annihilate them, was not difficult. "We shall fight the war as if there were no white paper," vowed Ben-Gurion, who lived in Palestine and traveled when possible throughout Europe during the war, "and we shall fight the white paper as if there were no war." He added that "this is our war no less than it is Britain's war or Russia's. Nothing that the rulers of the white paper may do will draw away our attention from the danger the world and the Jewish people have to face while Hitler exists. With our bodies, our souls, our capital, and our might, we shall participate in this holy war for we do not want, nor are we permitted, to let others do our work."

The Jews of Palestine made a large contribution to the British cause. Eager to join the struggle against the Nazis, some one hundred and thirty thousand of them registered as volunteers for military service during the first month of the war. By its end thirty-two thousand were on active duty with the British armed forces, having taken part in some of the hardest-fought campaigns.

In addition, in September 1944, the British war cabinet finally—after years of pressure from Jews in many parts of the world—risked Arab recriminations and sanctioned the establishment of the Jewish Brigade, an all-Jewish military corps of more than five thousand volunteers, flying its own Zionist

Opposite page: Men gather near a "Join the British Army" poster, Tel Aviv

flag with the yellow Star of David as its emblem, which fought against the German Army in Italy. And the Jews of Palestine gave more than manpower, contributing generous quantities of material goods to the British forces: food, clothing, medical supplies, military equipment, weapons, and other essential items.

On May 8, 1945, the Allies—Great Britain, France, the USSR, and the United States—announced the unconditional surrender of Germany. It was the end of the Second World War in Europe. According to Winston Churchill, who, as prime minister, had led Great Britain to its wartime triumph, the defeat of the Germans set off "the greatest outburst of joy in the history of mankind."

It was a tremendous victory and a cause for special rejoicing for the Jews of Europe, an end to many years during which one nation and its leader, Nazi Germany and Adolf Hitler, had tried to destroy them. Once the rejoicing had ended and they were freed of this threat to their lives, however, many of them had other challenges to face—above all, the search for a new home and often a new country in which to live.

These were the survivors, the "fortunate" Jews who had escaped death but spent the wartime years either hiding from their conquerors or imprisoned in concentration camps, where they were tortured, used for scientific experiments, or forced to work under inhuman conditions. At the time of their liberation, some were near death; it has been reported that of the sixty thousand Jews who walked out of the camps, at least twenty thousand died within a week. Others emerged from their hiding places debilitated and disheartened. The majority were too stunned to understand what had happened to them, and few were prepared to think of or plan for the future. In almost all cases, the joys

121

Opposite page: In Northern Italy, a member of the Jewish Brigade prepares to fire a shell bearing the Hebrew inscription "Souvenir for the Nazis"

Transport leaving the Bergen-Belsen concentration camp

of liberation were mixed with sadness as the survivors came to realize just how much—families, friends, homes, and communities—they had lost. Even the few who managed to return to their cities and towns were disappointed. Unable to pick up their lives where they had left them, they were constantly reminded of the years of humiliation, of unthinkable atrocities, and of tragedy. It would be impossible, most found, to build new lives on the ruins of the past. Even worse, a large number of the Jews who returned to their homes were welcomed not with compassion and apologies but with rage. Their former neighbors all too often blamed them for the war and complained that the Germans had not done a thorough enough job of eliminating them.

Of the many thousands of homeless Jews—or displaced persons—who wandered, lost, throughout Europe following the war, some managed to find refuge (as a small minority, along with many more non-Jewish homeless) in displaced-persons camps. These were transit camps that had been hastily built and organized by the United Nations Relief and Rehabilitation Administration, under the leadership of the United States. They were meant to be short-term solutions for the majority of the refugees, and they were just that for the non-Jews who were on their way home, but they were far more than that for the Jewish displaced persons (DPs). Since there was no Jewish state, no country the Jews could call their own, and no country that would welcome them, these transit camps became self-sustaining communities and rehabilitation centers where the refugees would have to wait for many months and even years before being able to make arrangements to move on to and establish themselves in other countries.

There was of course one solution for the refugees: immigration to Palestine. Though not yet their own state, it was the one land where they would be welcomed with the warmth and compassion they needed. No other countries had responded to their desperation. Even the British remained stubbornly committed to the termination of Jewish immigration to Palestine under the terms of the MacDonald White Paper. This was in spite of the assistance the Jews of Palestine had given them during the war and the hostility shown by the Palestinian Arabs, whose leader, the mufti of Jerusalem, was an outspoken supporter of the Nazis and had urged Muslims everywhere to rise up against the Allies. There had been some hope shortly before the end of the war, when

123

EXODUS-1947

In July 1947 a small, battered American ferry, the *President Garfield*, packed with some forty-five hundred Jewish refugees, set sail from southern France. Its destination was Palestine. Once at sea its name was changed to *Exodus-1947*. It became the symbol of the struggle for the right of free Jewish immigration into Palestine.

The ship was soon intercepted and "escorted" across the Mediterranean by six British destroyers and one cruiser. When the *Exodus-1947* was only a few miles from the Palestinian coast, the British approached it and attempted to board it. The refugees fought off the boarding party, until the British attacked with machine guns and gas bombs. Three Jews were killed and hundreds wounded. During the struggle the ship was in radio contact with the Haganah in Tel Aviv, and the exchange was later broadcast around the world.

Illegal immigrants from the ship *Exodus-1947* walk to a deportation ship in Haifa, 1947

The British search the belongings of children from *Exodus-1947* for weapons

The badly damaged vessel was towed into the port of Haifa and the passengers forced onto British ships to be returned to France. Following their arrival at the port of Marseille, the Jews, though offered asylum by the French government, refused to disembark, insisting that their destination was Palestine. The British vessels lay at anchor off the coast for approximately one month. During this time the thousands of refugees suffered from overcrowding, poor sanitary conditions, a shortage of food and water, and the brutal summer heat.

Finally the British decided to return them to internment camps in Germany. When the refugees again refused to disembark at the port of Hamburg, they were made to do so by British soldiers wielding clubs and hoses. Journalists who covered this dramatic struggle described to the entire world the cruelty and callousness of the British forces, and in so doing influenced world public opinion and won a stunning victory for the Zionist cause.

Britain's Labour Party, for many years supportive of the Jewish cause, came to power. But all hopes were abandoned when Ernest Bevin, Labour's foreign secretary, proved to be unequivocally opposed to the aspirations of the Jewish people. He made no attempt to hide his sympathy for the Arabs, whose friendship he carefully cultivated, not for humanitarian reasons but because they had access to military and naval installations and, above all, to oil, which was of major importance to the British.

In large part because of the attitude of the British, but also because of the world's indifference to the plight of the refugees, there was no Jewish state until three years after the end of the war. Before then, desperate, illegal measures were taken so that as many Jews as possible could reach Palestine. Groups, many organized under Ben-Gurion's supervision, were formed throughout Europe to recruit refugees and help organize their transportation to Palestine—secretly, by foot, by truck, by train, and finally by ship. These ingenious schemes were often successful, and thousands of men and women were able to reach their goal in this way. Because of a British naval blockade, however, many more failed to reach their destination. Of sixty-three ships that attempted to reach the shores of Palestine between April 1945 and January 1948, more than fifty were intercepted. The British were ruthless in their efforts to end the illegal immigration, turning back or even sinking boats filled with refugees. The Palestinian Jews, too, reacted angrily and violently at times to the British policies. In one extreme case, a Jewish terrorist group blew up a part of Jerusalem's King David Hotel, killing ninety-one Britons, Arabs, and Jews and injuring forty-five others. Another group was responsible for the hanging of two British soldiers. These acts of rage and frustration were vigorously deplored by Ben-Gurion and members of his party, who knew that they would only alienate the supporters that the Jews needed. Friends in every part of the world, especially the United States, sympathized with the refugees and rallied to the Zionist cause, protesting the brutal policies of the British.

The protests must have been effective for in February 1947 Bevin announced that the Palestine problem would be turned over to the United Nations, the successor to the League of Nations. The costs—in prestige as well as in the funds needed to support British troops in Palestine—were simply too high for the British to bear.

Word of Britain's planned evacuation of Palestine came as a great surprise, a welcome one for the Palestinian Jews. The United Nations acted quickly, and in April it set up an eleven-nation board to examine the problem. After several months of careful study and numerous interviews, the board recommended the termination of the British mandate and the partition of Palestine into two sovereign states, one Jewish and one Arab. It also urged that Jerusalem become an international city, administered by the United Nations.

The report was placed before the General Assembly of the United Nations and was adopted as Resolution 181. Thirty-three countries, including the United States and the Soviet Union, the two largest powers, supported it, thirteen were opposed, and ten, including Great Britain, abstained. A period of bickering and attempts at bargaining followed, with the Arabs and Zionists pitted against each other, but on November 29, 1947, the United Nations voted in favor of partition by a vote of 33 to 14.

It was a time of uninhibited joy for the Jewish people. Their dream was about to become a reality. A few months later, on May 14, 1948, with the last British troops prepared for departure, marking the official termination of the mandate, Ben-Gurion stood before a hastily convened provisional government at the Tel Aviv Museum to read the proclamation that declared the establishment of the state of Israel.

He was deeply moved. It was something he had dreamed of and fought for all his life, he remembered in an interview with Moshe Pearlman: "I thought, now at last we are responsible for our own destiny. It is ours to shape. We had been a minority element in scores of lands for almost two thousand years, our fate determined by others. . . . We had just lost six millions of our people, slaughtered by the Nazis. . . . For centuries we had been like flowers in a wood, some plucked by friendly hands, given water and nurtured, others trampled under foot and crushed. At no time could we be ourselves, enjoy independence, with the freedom to live a normal national life on our own soil, making our own decisions affecting our destiny. Now the hour had struck. We were independent once again."

Ben-Gurion's work was not finished, however. He continued to serve his people and his country—as prime minister, as a politician, and as a writer—until his death in 1973, at the age of eighty-seven.

Chaim Weizmann was unable to be in Tel Aviv for the proclamation ceremony on May 14. He was in New York, doing his best to see to it that all went well for his country on the diplomatic front. Though aged, ill, and half blind, he performed superbly, convincing President Harry S. Truman to support the new country wholeheartedly. Upon his return to what had become Israel, he was appointed president of the Provisional Council by Ben-Gurion and, in February 1949, was elected the first president of the state of Israel.

Weizmann died in his home at Rehovot on November 9, 1952, at the age of seventy-eight. Though he was physically unable to function effectively the last years of life, he will always be remembered for the many years of selfless struggle he waged for the independence of his country.

Opposite page: David Ben-Gurion just prior to reading the declaration of Israel's independence; he sits beneath a portrait of Theodor Herzl

Chaim Weizmann touches the cornerstone for the Weizmann Institute in Rehovot, Israel.

The promise had been fulfilled; the Jews had returned to their ancestral soil and regained their independence. The next day, however, their very existence was once again threatened. On May 15, the armies of five neighboring countries—Syria, Iraq, Transjordan, Lebanon, and Egypt—attacked the new republic.

Israel repelled this attack as it would the subsequent attacks that have continued, in different forms, to this day.

70 BCE	1492	1791	1860	1862
Exile of the Jews from Israel by Romans	Jews expelled from Spain	Emancipation of the Jews of France following the French Revolution	Birth of Theodor Herzl on May 2	Publication of Moses Hess's *Rome and Jerusalem*, a book advocating national liberation for the Jews by the creation of a Jewish state

1896	1897	1898	1903
Publication of Herzl's *Der Judenstaat* (*The Jewish State*)	First Zionist Congress in Basel, Switzerland	Herzl's visit to Palestine	British proposal for a Jewish homeland in East Africa

First Aliyah

1915	1917	1918	1919	1920
	Balfour Declaration, November 2	Armistice between Turkey and Great Britain and its allies, October 30	Treaty of Versailles, which ends World War I, signed June 28	Founding of Histadrut, General Confederation of Labor

Haganah founded |

Ben-Gurion in the United States

World War I   Third Aliyah

1932	1933	1936	1937	1939
	Adolf Hitler named chancellor of Germany		Peel Commission's plan for the partition of Palestine	MacDonald White Paper restricting Jewish immigration to Palestine

Arab revolt against the Zionists
and the British in Palestine

Fifth Aliyah   WWII

1874	1881	1882	1886	1894
Birth of Chaim Weizmann on November 27	Pogroms in Russia and in Poland	Formation of the movement Hovevei Zion ("lovers of Zion") as a result of the 1881 Russian pogroms	Birth of David Ben-Gurion, né David Green, on October 10	Dreyfus trial

First Aliyah

1904	1906	1908	1909	1914
Death of Herzl on July 3	Arrival of Ben-Gurion in Palestine on September 7	Founding of Degania, the first kibbutz	Founding of Tel Aviv Founding of Hashomer	Declaration of war by Great Britain on Germany, August 4

Second Aliyah   WWI

1922	1923	1924	1925	1929
Formalization of the British mandate for Palestine by the League of Nations on July 24			Opening of Hebrew University	Arab rioting throughout Palestine and clashes between Arabs and Jews Founding of the socialist political party Mapai

Third Aliyah   Fourth Aliyah

1944	1945	1947	1948
Jewish Brigade formed and attached to Royal Army	Liberation of extermination camps	United Nations resolution for the partition of Palestine	Proclamation of independence of the state of Israel

World War II and the Holocaust

FOR FURTHER READING

Ausubel, Nathan. *Pictorial History of the Jewish People.* New York: Crown Publishers, 1953.

Bauer, Yehuda. *Flight and Resistance: Bricah.* New York: Random House, 1970.

Bein, Alex. *Theodor Herzl.* New York and Philadelphia: Meridian, Jewish Publication Society, 1962.

Ben-Gurion, David. *Israel: Years of Challenge.* New York: Holt, Rinehart and Winston, 1963.

————*Memoirs.* New York and Cleveland: World, 1970.

Blumberg, H. M. *Weizmann: His Life and Times.* New York: St. Martin's Press, 1975.

Crossman, Richard H. S. *A Nation Reborn.* New York: Atheneum, 1960.

Dawidowicz, Lucy S. *The War Against the Jews, 1933–1945.* New York: Holt, Rinehart and Winston, 1975.

Eban, Abba. *Heritage: Civilization and the Jews.* New York: Summit Books, 1984.

Elon, Amos. *Herzl.* New York: Holt, Rinehart and Winston, 1975.

Gilbert, Martin. *The Holocaust: A History of the Jews of Europe During the Second World War.* New York: Holt, Rinehart and Winston, 1985.

Hertzberg, Arthur, ed. *The Zionist Idea: A Historical Analysis and Reader.* Garden City, New York: Doubleday, 1959.

Herzl, Theodor. *The Jewish State (Der Judenstaat).* New York: Herzl Press, 1970.

Johnson, Paul. *A History of the Jews.* New York: Harper & Row, 1987.

Kurzman, Dan. *Ben-Gurion: Prophet of Fire.* New York: Simon and Schuster, 1983.

Laqueur, Walter. *A History of Zionism*. New York: Schocken Books, 1976.

Lowenthal, Marvin, ed. *The Diaries of Theodor Herzl*. New York: The Dial Press, 1956.

Memmi, Albert. *The Liberation of the Jew*. New York: The Orion Press, 1966.

Patai, Raphael, ed. *Encyclopedia of Zionism and Israel*. New York: Herzl Press/McGraw-Hill, 1971.

Pawel, Ernst. *The Labyrinth of Exile: A Life of Theodor Herzl*. New York: Farrar, Straus and Giroux, 1989.

Pearlman, Moshe. *Ben-Gurion Looks Back*. London: Weidenfeld and Nicolson, 1965.

Rose, Norman. *Chaim Weizmann*. New York: Viking, 1986.

Sachar, Abram Leon. *A History of the Jews*. New York: Alfred A. Knopf, 1964.

Sachar, Howard M. *A History of Israel*. New York: Alfred A. Knopf, 1976.

———*Aliyah: The Peoples of Israel*. New York and Cleveland: World, 1964.

Sanders, Ronald. *The High Walls of Jerusalem*. New York: Holt, Rinehart and Winston, 1983.

Seltzer, Robert M. *Jewish People, Jewish Thought: The Jewish Experience in History*. New York: Macmillan, 1980.

Sherman, A. J. *Mandate Days: British Lives in Palestine, 1918–1948*. Baltimore and London: Johns Hopkins University Press, 1997.

Shlaim, Avi. *War and Peace in the Middle East*. New York: Penguin Books, 1995.

Shulman, Abraham. *Coming Home to Zion*. Garden City, New York: Doubleday, 1979.

St. John, Robert. *Ben-Gurion.* Garden City, New York: Doubleday, 1971.

Teveth, Shabtai. *Ben-Gurion and the Palestinian Arabs.* New York: Oxford University Press, 1985.

————*Ben-Gurion and the Holocaust.* New York: Harcourt Brace, 1996.

Weisgal, Meyer. *Meyer Weisgal . . . so far: an Autobiography.* New York: Random House, 1971.

Weizmann, Chaim. *Trial and Error.* New York: Harper & Row, 1949.

Weizmann, Vera. *The Impossible Takes Longer.* New York: Harper & Row, 1967.

Zweig, Stefan. *The World of Yesterday.* New York: Viking Press, 1945.

ACKNOWLEDGMENTS

I am indebted to a number of men and women who have given generously of their time and knowledge in the course of my work on this book, and it gives me great pleasure to acknowledge this debt. Among those who assisted me were: Jesse Cohen, Ronald Columbus, Rebecca Davis, Virginia Duncan, Caryn Faber, Susan Heller, Susan Hirschman, Aliza Kaplan, Dr. Alexander Kirschenbaum, Maria Rosenbloom, Professor Robert M. Seltzer, and Ann Shore.

A few words of special thanks to Avi Jezer, a scholar and educator, whose contribution to this book cannot be overstated. He read the manuscript thoroughly and offered intelligent and perceptive suggestions which enabled me to improve it.

I am profoundly grateful to my wife, Paola, and our son, Daniel, who, as always, sustained and encouraged me from the beginning of this project to its conclusion.

PHOTO CREDITS

The scope of this volume made it occasionally difficult—despite sincere and sustained effort—to locate photographers and/or their executors. The author regrets any omissions or errors, and will make any necessary corrections in subsequent printings.

Permission to reprint copyrighted material is gratefully acknowledged to the following:

Government Press Office of the State of Israel for permission to print:
Title page and pages 23, 25, 40, 41, 43, 46, 47, 48, 50, 52, 87, 95, 97, 99, 102, 109, 116, 124, and 125 photographs by unknown photographers
Pages 14, 73 (top), 75, 86, 89, 105, and 119 photographs by Zoltan Kluger
Page 18 photograph by Ya'acov Sa'ar
Page 90 photograph by David Eldan
Page 129 photograph by Frank Shershel
Page 130 photograph by Hans Pinn

Yaffa Eliach Shtetl Collection for permission to print photographs on:
Pages 73 (bottom), 77, 83, and 114

Archives of the YIVO Institute for Jewish Research, New York, for permission to print photographs on:
Pages 74–75, 107, 120, and 122

INDEX

Page references to photos are in *italics*.

139